LINEAGE

LINEAGE

*Poems and Prose
of three Generations*

William Silver Jennings,
Robert Kimmel Jennings,
and
Lane Eaton Jennings

Library of Congress Control Number: 2012908085
ISBN: Hardcover   978-1-4691-9976-4
                 Softcover   978-1-4691-9975-7
                 Ebook   978-1-4691-9977-1

This book was printed in the United States of America.

To order additional copies of this book, contact:
Xlibris Corporation
1-888-795-4274
www.Xlibris.com
Orders@Xlibris.com
113791

LINEAGE:

Writers of Three Generations

CONTENTS

*=previously published

Writings by **Robert Kimmel Jennings** (1912-1996)

*=previously published

Writings by **Lane Eaton Jennings** (b. 1944)

*=previously published

Exchanges and Collaborations:
Cross-Generational Conversations and Parallels in Verse

To Irene,
Edith, Cheryl,
And others unnamed
Who drew our love
And were
Our inspiration

Best pals. Bob Jennings and his little boy, ca. 1950

Introduction

On the back cover of this book are pictures of three young men, each bright with promise and ready to take on the world. They each set out at different times in different directions. The first one, in the early 1900s, headed west toward the American frontier. The second, in the depths of the Depression, traveled east toward economic opportunity. The third, in the mid-1960s, flew off across the ocean to discover what was new and different from the world he knew. Each had their adventures and excitements, triumphs and setbacks, joys and griefs. And, I think it is fair to say, they each achieved their goals—though not quite in the ways they had expected.

All three of these young men are gone now—two dead, and one well into late middle age. All three loved deeply, married, and two each had an only child, a boy, to carry on the family name. And all of them were writers: the first two not full-time professionals, but writing mainly for their own amusement or, now and then, to earn a little extra money. The third, however had grander ambitions. Writers were his heroes from an early age, and he aspired someday to be one of them himself—he thought of them as his extended family. (And a good thing, too, considering that he did *not* have any children of his own, and has thus effectively consigned his hereditary line to ultimate extinction.)

The pages that follow contain examples of each man's writing in prose and verse. These include one sample each of something written "on the job," a dozen or so poems, and a couple stories. Then there is a section in which generations intentionally or accidentally interact—poem and answering poem, or lines originally penned by one writer that were later expanded or amended by another. Closing the book, you'll find a brief bibliography of works by these authors available in print or online, plus an index listing the book's contents by title and first line.

If anything you find here entertains or amuses you, moves you, or stimulates your thoughts in new directions, please convey this to the living co-author (reachable online at *lanejen@aol.com*). He, and his forebears, will be most gratified.

—Lane Jennings Columbia, MD
10 April 2012

WILLIAM SILVER JENNINGS

Born in 1877, raised on an Ohio farm, Quaker, the son of a Civil War soldier wounded at Gettysburg, William Silver Jennings attended Ohio State University, earning a BA, and MA in Education. In 1910 he married Irene Kimmel and went west with his young wife to become the first Superintendent of Schools in Cody, Wyoming. When, two years later, Irene died in childbirth delivering their son Robert, William returned home to Eaton, Ohio. Not long after, he moved to Indiana where taught high school in Indianapolis. He was also a farmer, and local news correspondent, who wrote articles, stories, and poems. He died of a sudden heart attack in 1924.

Poems by William Silver Jennings

PIPE LURE

BOYHOOD

Sitting alone in a big bare barn,
On an upturned basket seat,
Jacket and jumper of homespun yarn,
Dirty and naked feet;
     Puff, puff, puff,
The corn-silk smoke is fair,
With eyes fixed fast on the thin blue bands,
And the stem held tight in his chubby hands,
Is there aught that the small head understands
In the charm that holds him there?

YOUTH

Strolling around the campus grounds
Where the shady paths are long,
And the strident sound of the class bell drowns
In the breeze and the tree top's song;
     Puff, puff, puff,
While life is young and fair,
The meerschaum brings its throng of dreams,
Of name and fame, the round it teems
Ambition's brood, while purpose beams
Bright in the summer air.

MANHOOD

After his daily bread he earns
Home to the nest at night,
Quiet and peace where the hearth fire burns
Cheery and warm and bright.
       Puff, puff, puff,
The briar wood's scent is rife,
Trouble and care have winged away,
Vanished the fears of another day,
Here with the mother and babe at play,
Sweet is the joy of life.

AGE

A big fire-place and a rocking chair,
And a corn-cob pipe aglow,
A wrinkled face and whitened hair,
And thoughts of the long ago.
       Puff, puff, puff,
While circling spirals rise,
A face peers out from the smoky haze,
A fair sweet face of the by-gone days,
Beckoning him through the misty maze
To a saintly paradise.

CORN KING

Blessings on thee, little man,
    Farmer boy with cheeks of tan,
With thy record breaking crop
    Putting over one on pop.

Thou hast mastered all the lore
    Of the Ag. Department's store,
Studying in the stilly night
    By the yellow coal oil light.

In the summer's burning sun
    Thou didst labor much alone,
Weeding all the weary rows,
    Chasing off the pesky crows.

Boreas tried with thee his steel,
    Sought to break thy sturdy will;
But the bitter frosty morn
    Found thee up and shucking corn.

Ceres lost her heart to thee,
    Knight of modern chivalry,
And Apollo never showed
    Yields to equal those thou growed.

To the White House hie thee then,
    Sit thee with the best of men,
And, returning, teach thy pop
    How to raise a better crop.

TO A ROMAN BEAUTY APPLE

When shines the sun so ardent on the meadows,
And in the hay the field hands do their duty,
I seek the orchard's green refreshing shadows,
And taste the sweetness of the Roman Beauty.

Like mists of morning, vanish then my sorrows,
For nature is a nurse of rarest measure;
A balm to heartache, weariness and hunger,
I find my mellow, luscious Roman treasure.

Then thou, O Beauty, writest to thy credit
One soul's sweet comfort and one palate's pleasure
To balance, 'gainst the debit on thy ledger,
Some boy's encounter with too green a treasure.

Thy ways are modest and thy gifts unlettered
And all thy recompense for faithful duty
Is but to know that thou hast given pleasure
To God's own creatures, blessed Roman Beauty.

A TRYST

We sat beneath the linden tree
Where fragrant south winds breathed perfume
Of mignonette, of locust bloom,
Of mint and rosemary.

The little cheek so near my face,
Whose dainty curve no pen can sing,
Whose roseate blush no brush can swing,
My fingers did embrace.

And oft a lover's true caress,
A lover's kiss untarnished,
Upon that velvet amber-red
My lips did fondly press.

The furry forager scampering by
Stopped short with paws upraised to list,
The while we kept our silent tryst,
My little love and I.

The carping crickets paused to hear,
Their music ceased in the linden boughs
While oft I whispered tender vows
Unto . . . my Meerschaum dear.

PHYLLIS HATH MY HEART IN TOW

Phyllis hath my heart in tow
    And my fancy lingers
On the rustle of her dress,
On her grace and comeliness,
E'en upon the loveliness
    Of her slender fingers;
Straight hath Cupid drawn his bow—
Phyllis hath my heart in tow.

In the eve and in the morn,
    In the noontide beaming,
Think, I must, of Phyllis fair,
See, I must, her golden hair,
Hear her laughter everywhere
    And I'm ever dreaming
Gentle dreams of Phyllis, born
All the night till rosy morn.

Tender light is in her eye,
    Like the light that flashes
Where the sunbeams kiss a star
In the midnight skies afar
Naught is there the grace to mar
    'Neath her drooping lashes.
Visions fair of Phyllis rise
Everywhere before my eyes.

Surely is my heart in tow,
    But my hopes are shattered;
To my fond request today
Phyllis fair hath said me nay,
Given naught but laughter gay
    Thought it little mattered,
I shall try tomorrow, though;
Phyllis hath my heart in tow.

MAYTIME

One day in May the sun shone fair,
The scent of spring was in the air,
And by the spring there wandered there
Daphne and Damon, loving pair,
    That day
        In May.

Wandered so slow and carelessly,
Walking as close as close could be;
Gazing upon the ground was she,
Gazing upon the ground was he,
    That day
        In May.

Big Damon's curly head bent low
As in a gentle voice and slow
He whispered "Daphne, don't you know
Your promise made so long ago?
    Some day
        Next May."

Sweet Daphne's dimpled cheek grew red;
Could it have been what Damon said,
Or what the breezes murmured,
Or just the bluebird overhead,
    That day
        In May.

Nobody else was there to see,
Yet I know what the bird told me,
For bird and breeze they both agree
That Daphne answered roguishly
    "'Tis May
        Today!"

WINTER NIGHT

The night is cold, and night winds bold
Are howling through the sky,
And people go with heads bent low
And collars standing high.
        But we have peace and cheer, my dear
        And light and warmth are here, my dear:
                Cupid, and you, and I.

The storm doth rave upon the wave
And battle with the light,
And God must care for those who dare
To ride the sea tonight.
        But we are safe from harm, my dear
        No need for any 'larm, my dear,
                While our fire burns so bright.

Then let it blow, both loud and low,
And tear the drifts apart,
And let it cold and colder grow
With every freshening start;
        For wood is piled within, my dear
        And meal is in the bin, my dear,
                And love is in the heart.

[*I like to imagine WSJ wrote this out in Cody, Wyoming where he and his wife Irene lived happily—if briefly—together.*—LJ]

THE PASSING STORM

A darkening sun and a rumble
A frown on the western sky,
A whirling of dust in the rushing wind.
And big drops rattling by,
A roar of the gale in the forest,
With strong oaks bending low,
A flash, a crash, and a quivering wreck,
For a century's growth to show.

'twas only the laws of nature,
Pressures and currents and all—
But I saw the might of a ruling hand,
And I heard a wondrous call;
'twas God in his wonderful heaven,
Speaking in accents clear;
Majesty, glory, and power were his,
Mine was the listening ear.

A rift in the western curtain,
A bright ray streaming through,
Glory of crimson, purple and gold,
A smell of the wet earth, too,
The fragrance of honey locust,
Of lilacs bursting free,
A twittering under the dripping eaves,
And happiness for me.

'twas only the laws of nature,
Refraction, spectrums and things,
With a little of warmth and moisture,
A growing and flutter of wings;
But I saw the face of Jesus,
Radiant, happy and bright,
And I caught the sound of a seraph song
Out of the realms of light.

THE MOUNTAINS (Irene)

You westward gazed with weary eyes
To where the purple mountains rise
All crowned with sunset glow.
You marked the homeward eagle's flight
Into the wondrous depths of light;
Ah love, 'twas heaven opening bright;
You could not choose but go.

In vain I prayed to follow there;
Not mine the distant vision fair;
All lonely must I stay.
Yet as I watch the day depart
The mountains shed with magic art
Their solemn peace into my heart,
And I can bide the day.

WHEN I AM GONE

When I am gone
I want no weight of garlands
Clustered there,
Scenting the oppressive air
With cloying fragrance, as of heavy heart;
But draw the blinds apart,
Let God's sweet sun shine in,
Let hope of mortal morning there begin,
Let birds sing cheerily, and children laugh,
The thirsty soul that was, has gone to quaff
Its meed of wine.
Therefore let joy be thine
When I am gone.

When I am gone
I want no quivering sigh,
No sobbing line,
"What grievous loss is mine."
But rather, steadfast courage to turn again
Indifferent to pain,
And cry "What blessed joy was this!
What wondrous cup my lips have pressed to kiss!
What rapture thou didst give!
Should joy be less now than when thou didst live?"
So happy be,
And do not weep for me
When I am gone.

Stories by William Silver Jennings

Adoniram Retreats (1915)

By William S. Jennings

Adoniram trod gingerly, lifting his bare feet high and planting them carefully between the bunches of short, sharp stubble. The heavy water-jug tugged at the strap which encircled his wrist, and the little drops of condensed moisture ran from its cool sides and trickled down the boy's dusty calves, leaving clean furrows where they passed.

A sweating jug was a sure sign of rain. This was as much an unquestioned article of Adoniram's creed as that bumblebees are always angry before a storm, and that, as every boy knows, is the ABC of knowledge. The boy paused, set down the heavy jug, and regarded the appearance of the sky. The sun was brazen and the air sultry. He lifted the jug to his lips and drank. Then he poured a copious bath on his feet; it was cool and pleasant. The jug was lighter now, and the voice of the hired man, calling to his team in the upper meadow, recalled him to duty, so he proceeded on his way.

As he moved slowly through the stubble field, his practiced eye noted here and there certain tufts of brown sedge nestled close to the ground. At one of these, he finally paused, and setting down the jug, peered cautiously about for signs of life. Tentatively he prodded the mass with his bee-shingle. For Adoniram was no more to be found without his bee-shingle in haying time than was ever bold troubadour swordless, or cowboy of the Diamond Story series wanting pistol.

The first gentle poke brought results, and an irate yellow resident came tumbling out to investigate the intrusion. Being discreet as well as valiant, the boy backed off a few steps, and poised his weapon for combat, but the adversary did not take wing. Instead, he climbed to the top of a clump of stubble, tumbled off, and retired again within his domicile.

Adoniram reflected. The hired man was thirsty; that was a matter of course. Hired men were *always* thirsty. On the other hand, here was a nest just prime. There must be honey in that nest; and anyway, bumblebees are bumblebees, and the blood of nine years is ever hot for battle with the hereditary foe. But again the hired man's voice drifted in on the still afternoon air, with the clatter of the mower. Thus prompted to duty once again the boy decided he would just stir things up a bit by way of challenge, then hasten on his way. Some other time he would return and lick the whole nest single handed.

Having made this virtuous resolve, he stooped, picked up a large clod carefully, and launched it at the nest. The result surpassed his fondest expectations. Out from the brown tuft of sedge poured the whole tribe. It seemed to Adoniram that he had never seen so many bumblebees at once in all his wide experience. A small cloud of them hovered low over the nest, and others crawled in the grass, seeking the source of the earthquake that had shaken their habitation. One hovered about the jug and paused near the open mouth, attracted by the resonant echo of its own buzzing. But a few, flying in a wider circle, spied the animated person of their foe and at once gave chase.

As Adoniram was valorous, he was likewise a good judge of odds, and realizing at once the disadvantage of numbers, he beat a quick retreat. As he ran, he swung once, twice, over his head and heard the gratifying splat that meant the death of a bee. But the pursuit continued. With good strategy the enemy harassed the rear of the fleeing force, and even as the boy caught one adversary on the point of his weapon, another of the band spied a weak spot in his armor—that is to say a hole in his trousers.

Adoniram had forgotten that hole. His father had said it proved that the boy was doing entirely too much sitting around for a busy family, and his mother had remarked that she must sew it up right away, then being busy, she had neglected it. Adoniram now regretted that neglect.

Having located the enemy's vulnerable spot, the pursuing antagonist deftly inserted a barbed dart deep into the sunburned skin beneath, upon which Adoniram instantly developed a burst of speed that surprised even himself, and left his pursuers far in the rear. He continued his retreat to the meadow fence, and there paused to assure himself that the pursuit was abandoned. Though his full flight had been precipitous, it had been conducted in fairly good order, bringing off the artillery, and the boy now deposited his shingle in the fence corner and set to work to give first aid to the wounded. The sting was burning like fury, and Adoniram recalled a remedy much recommended by the hired man.

A small handful of earth and modicum of saliva yielded the required amount of mud. This he plastered on the swelling, and stood about to await some cessation of the pain. His faith was great, though he had never tried the remedy, his previous stings having been treated by his mother with soda and water and a bandage.

After long waiting, and much uneasiness on the part of the patient, together with some tears, the pain settled down to a dull ache, and now thoroughly chastened in body and spirit, the boy thought once more of his errand and made a careful reconnaissance. Being assured that the bees had subsided, Adoniram cautiously secured his jug, and his straw hat which had been abandoned in flight, and proceeded on his way.

The hired man *was* thirsty. "Goodness, boy, do you think I'm one o' them gi-raffs, that c'n go all week without water?" was his greeting.

Adoniram tried to look contrite, and succeeded fairly well, sorrow and pain being very near neighbors, if not relatives. "Got stung crossing the lower meadow," he explained tersely.

"Did you put some mud on it? Nothin' like mud fer a sting," offered the hired man solicitously.

"Yep," Adoniram assured him, and assumed the unconcern best calculated to forestall further inquiry as to the location of his injury, for the hired man had a way of never forgetting a joke, the boy knew. This ruse, or thirst alone, succeeded and the hired man, climbing down from his seat, paused only to push back his had and mop his brow before uttering the prelude of every drink in the field: "Boy, what'll you gimme if I drink out o' this jug with one hand?"

Adoniram grinned appreciation, knowing well that no further inducement was needed or expected. Holding his hat in his left hand, the hired man grasped the jug handle with his right. Then, with a quick backward turn of the wrist, he swung the jug to the upper surface of his bent elbow and elevated it to his face. The mouth of the jug was large, but larger still was that of the hired man, and hired men in the field do not drink—they guzzle.

And so it was that the solitary occupant of the jug, at this moment clinging bravely to the surface within, found its egress from that dark cistern suddenly made easy, and in its hasty exit encountered first the hired man's tongue, which partly blocked the entrance to regulate the flow.

Now, nothing can possibly get madder that a wet bumblebee—not even a thirsty hired man thwarted in his drink. Adoniram was startled at the suddenness with which the jug flew over the stubble. He was transfixed by the vigor with which the hire man spat, and paralyzed by the violence with which he yelled.

"Holy Moses, kid, What d'ya DO?"

At this, the spell broke, and for the second time that day, Adoniram beat a sudden and swift retreat, nor did he pause till he had gained the shelter of his mother's kitchen.

The hired man did not appear at supper that evening. Also Adoniram did not loiter at table when the meal was done, but edged from his chair and quickly left the kitchen by the back door.

Rounding the house, he unexpectedly encountered the hired man, perched gloomily on the edge of the porch, staring into space. Adoniram hesitated, leaned against the house, and rubbed one great toe sympathetically up and down the opposite shin.

"Did," the boy began solicitously, "did you put some *mud* on it?"

The hired man made no retort, but cast one awful, wilting, withering look at his questioner.

For the third time, Adoniram retreated.

French Fried (ca. 1918)

By William Silver Jennings

Jerry McCarty was hungry; hungrier than he had ever been in his life. He could not recall, in fact, that real necessity had ever 'til now deprived him of a single meal, for in boyhood the pantry and the warming oven at home had always been there to save him when he had felt starvation approaching, and at college, the boarding house and the handy lunchroom had served him well.

As his mind dwelt on the good things he had known, the boy's hunger increased, but his deep thrust hands discovered not so much as a pocket knife that might be exchanged for the price of a ham sandwich; nothing, in fact but a few bits of cardboard, and he shivered and wished for the overcoat he had left back in Illinois. The pawn ticket was a poor substitute now, though the exchange had enabled him to travel somewhat farther. Similarly, watch and suitcase had remained in St. Louis where he had last dined after hunting all day in vain for a job.

Jerry supposed there must be an amusing side to that westward trail strewn with his small belongings and wearing apparel, but just now he couldn't see it. The trip was, to be sure, not exactly as he had imagined it on that commencement day when he had declared in favor of seeing the world a bit, instead of accepting the proffered place in his Uncle Abner's law office. He was not yet sure whether it had been censure or regret that had tinged his uncle's crisp reply, "Go to it, then, and when you've seen it come back and tell me what it looks like. I've been too busy to go see it myself. But it's on your own resources you go, remember that." At the time this had sounded like a challenge. The sporting strain in the young collegian rose to the challenge and he was soon off carrying only hand baggage.

Down in the railroad yards below the bridge on which the boy was standing, a line of men attracted his attention. They were waiting beside one of a long string of Pullman cars, and to Jerry they looked like vagabonds. It suggested a bread line, but that could scarcely be in such a place. Perhaps, he thought, there were jobs to be had down there.

Jerry had tramped the streets since his arrival on an early morning freight. There were no sidewalks to be swept, no windows to be washed. Even his offer to carry a handbag from the station for an incoming passenger had failed miserably. He had not yet reached the stage of hoboism where begging is easy. That might come in time, but as yet he was too fresh from college, from his home life, and from eastern standards of conduct.

With a dull hope and a mild curiosity he descended and approached the straggling line. "What's up?" he inquired of the rearmost man.

"Takin' on men for dining car service." Was the reply, and Jerry silently fell in line behind.

When the Coast Range Limited pulled out of Denver that midnight, it carried among others up forward, Jerry McCarty, a hobo no longer but a regularly enrolled employee of the great railroad company, in the humble but necessary position of Fourth Class Cook. You go on duty at Baker's Junction," the agent had said, scanning him closely meanwhile. "They pick up a diner there. Report to the chef. That's all."

The ride to Baker's Junction was a long one. Jerry made it on his nerve; that and the pride of the McCartys, which kept him from mentioning hunger to any of his traveling companions who were also to report at various places along the line, all of whom seemed in good spirits and some of whom even had money they could spend at the wayside stations.

Thus it was a somewhat weak and woebegone Fourth Class Cook who eventually reported to the chef in the dining car at Bakers Junction.

"Ever do any cookin'?" inquired that individual as he regarded his new recruit closely.

"Not a bit," Jerry was obliged to confess. He was on the point of adding "Sir." But repressed the impulse.

"Ever peel p'tatoes? Wash any dishes?"

With inward trepidation, the recruit admitted limited experience at both these tasks, and the chef smiled broadly, revealing a fine set of ivories and a jovial disposition at the same time. "That's th' job, boy; that's a Fo'th Class Cook." Then, after a keen glance at his visitor he dived into the cupboard. "Looky here, boy, you get busy with these right now," he commanded emerging and setting forth a luscious brown pie, a loaf of bread, fresh butter, and a jug of milk.

Jerry got busy.

Carter City lies high up in the foothills of the Rockies. It is the last sizeable station on the eastern side of the long climb which the Limited makes to clear the backbone of the continent. Here the tired engine goes clanking gladly off to its stable while two mammoth steel beasts move grandly out to be hitched up for the big pull to the top, and here the weary passengers stretch their cramped legs up and down the long platform, marveling at their first real close-up of snow-capped peaks, and glorying in the stimulus of rarified mountain air.

It was here that Jerry McCarty, veteran Fourth Class Cook by virtue of five hours experience stood enthralled, scanning the trappings of a bunch of saddle ponies and their bechapped and bespurred riders. This was his first introduction to the West of his boyhood dreams, and, spellbound, he reveled in the rare thrill of the sight until a clanging bell ahead and the conductor's long-drawn "Bo-o-o-o-ard" disturbed his trance. Whistling happily the boy swung aboard and was engrossed in his pots and pans when the chef entered the tiny kitchen and looked at him sharply.

"Mac, where's the spuds?" he inquired?

A panic of remorse and surprise drove the color from Jerry's countenance. "Oh my gosh, Cook, I entirely forgot to get out those potatoes."

The ready humor of the genial chef failed on this occasion. In a short time he must be ready to serve French fried potatoes according to the bill of fare already distributed throughout the train, and experience told him that a large percentage of passengers would be sure to order that particular item. Besides he had been most explicit in his orders to this new recruit to get out a bag of potatoes from the provision tank under the car when the train stopped at Carter City. "That's the only chance we got to get 'em," he had warned and even added "Don't forget it!" to which Jerry had replied reassuringly, "All right, Cook."

The chef gave one despairing groan. Then, with a shrug of his broad shoulders and a gesture of finality, he said, "Well. They's just one thing to be done now. Git the rope ladder an' climb down off'n th' roof."

Jerry stared, incredulous. He would dare anything to save his chief the displeasure of the powers, but this suggestion he regarded as suicidal. He was hesitating uncertainly when Harley, the Second Cook, passing near him spoke a few words in a low voice, ending with "We've all had to do it sometimes. Don't worry. I'll help you."

In the cupboard Jerry found a rope ladder somewhat worn but still apparently strong, and a wicker basket. He followed Harley into the front vestibule to open the side door and, imitating the other's use of the foot and hand holds on the side of the car, soon arrived on the roof of the dining car just behind his companion.

The car was rocking and swaying over the rough roadbed which wound a torturous course through the hills. Unaccustomed to the experience, the two young men were obliged to crawl on their hands and knees, clinging tightly all the while, until they arrived at the midpoint of the car, where a pair of hooks projected from the roof on either side of the ventilator. Harley took the ladder and, making one end fast, tossed the other out and down. "You pass 'em up," he said briefly; "and I'll take 'em."

Jerry embraced the ventilator roof fondly, tightly, with a sort of 'goodbye-forever' strangle-hold, while he eased his legs outward and felt for a foothold on the ladder. The half-inch ropes seemed terribly frail supports for his hundred and thirty-five pounds. As he retreated slowly, step by step, down from the cornice, the drunkenly swaying car roof suddenly became a most desirable resting place, while the reeling earth beneath him seemed to be clanging and crashing and reaching up with eager jaws to seize his dangling legs.

Soon he was on the level of the car windows. How sweetly secure the white dining tables inside looked, all dressed with glittering silver! There was no one within however to say goodbye. He continued gingerly climbing downward.

His feet were below the floor level now, and the ladder showed a disconcerting tendency to swing underneath the car. Glancing down, Jerry saw the loose ends of rope sweeping the ties that flashed past in a dizzying stream. He must keep his feet free of those ties, no doubt of that. He found it necessary to use force in persuading them to take the last few steps downward. Some invisible power seemed to urge him back, but opposed to it were the frowning chef and the need for French fried potatoes, that could not be resisted.

The boy clung tightly with his left hand while, with his right, he extracted the key from deep in his pocket. He was had to bend far over to reach the storage compartment. Just as he did so, the lower end of the ladder swung out and his feet slipped on their rest. For a moment his dangling form tossed like a scarecrow in the wind.

Breathless and white, he regained his balance and straightened on the ladder. Then he persuaded his reluctant legs to descend one more step, two steps, nearer the savagely rushing tide of ragged ties. Keeping his feet carefully beneath him, he slowly bent his knees, crouching lower and lower until he could see the lock on the compartment door.

Time and again he thrust unsteadily with the key until at last it entered the lock, the door yielded, and opening out and down, formed a shelf on which he could rest his basket and steady his swinging body.

The sack of potatoes was there. But it was far too big to lift, and it was sewn up tight. Using the key, Jerry worked one end of the string loose and opened the sack far enough to slip his hand inside. Working rapidly, he filled the basket.

Now for the return! Going up had to be easier; much easier, for there were no flying crossties above his head.

Shifting his weight to his other hand, the boy swung his left arm a few times to loosen the cramped muscles then gripped the handle of the now-heavy basket and swung it up off the shelf. He solved the problem of shutting the door by leaving it open. If he got back alive he would be the first one off the train when it stopped. And if he didn't, it wouldn't matter.

As he straightened up with his burden, the car entered a sharp curve and, careened, swinging the ladder far out from its side, while the wind caught and turned him half about. A warning shout came from above, and Jerry glimpsed a telegraph pole flashing to meet him. There was a crash. Potatoes rained on the right of way, and only a fragment of the basket hung to the arm of the boy as his head banged hard against the now perpendicular side of the dining car.

Dazed and gasping for breath, he hung there an instant, dumbly trying to decide if he were dead or only fatally crushed, while the train rumbled hollowly out onto the high trestle bridge that spans Clearwater Canyon. He tightened his grip on the rope ladder and held grimly on until the deep chasm below and passed and the wheels were clicking over solid ground again.

Satisfied at last that he was unhurt, but with shaking knees and trembling breath, he tried hard to resist the temptation to drop off and instead thought only of potatoes.

"Come on up," shouted Harley.

"No I won't. Not without the spuds," called Jerry with a resolution he did not feel, and slowly descended once more to the level of the storage bin.

With his free hand he scooped and rolled potatoes from the open bag until it was considerably more than half emptied. Then he dragged it forth, twisting the loose end deftly about his left arm, and, holding the burden close against his side, hastened back up the ladder.

Harley reached down from above, took the bag, and had just helped him back up on the roof when a long drawn whistle ahead gave warning. "Lie down!" Harley shouted frantically. Before imitating his companion and throwing himself face down beside the ventilator and clinging there desperately, Jerry had just time to realize that the big engines two cars ahead were entering a hole in the mountain wall; a hole which looked to be several sizes smaller than the engines themselves.

Sudden blackness swallowed them and a smother of thick hot smoke scorched their lungs. Jerry coughed hard, then, burying his face in his sleeve, he bit tightly and held his breath. Hot cinders rained down burning into his flesh. His lungs were bursting , but he dared not breathe in the choking sulfurous gas.

There was no knowing how long the tunnel might be. It seemed ages that he lay there. Jerry's temples throbbed, his ears rang with tumult. Tons of weight were crushing his breast. Then suddenly the crashing of the train became a muffled, far-off murmur, his grasp on the ventilator loosened, his body relaxed, his mouth opened and he drew in a long, gasping breath.

Harley turned and looked at Jerry.

"You all right?"

Jerry nodded. "You?"

For answer, Harley just grinned and held aloft the soot-stained sack partly filled with fine large, smooth Irish potatoes.

*   *   *

In the dining car that noon the first comer, an overdressed, bejeweled lady of mature years and generous figure, summoned the head waiter and imperiously demanded to know why her French fried potatoes were so slow in coming.

"They're frying right now, Madame," he assured her. "I will hurry them to you immediately. The boys were a trifle late getting them prepared, I'm sorry to say."

"Well, 'the boys,' should be given a lesson. I shall certainly complain to the authorities of such abominably slow service. It's inexcusable!"

"Yes, ma'm," soothed the waiter.

The Trouble Shooter (ca. 1918)

By William S. Jennings

We were sitting in the dynamo room of the power plant at Echo Falls when the engineer told me the story. The roar of the falls outside and the soughing of wind in the pine trees blended with the soft whirr of the big dynamos till it seemed that the whole valley was filled with some strange weird music. The engineer had been telling me of the line of high tension cables and telephone wires that ran on steel towers over the mountain range to Bernard eight miles away, carrying the electric current to that city. "T'was a big job," he said, "to build that line. And 'tis a big job to keep it up. There's always trouble of some sort, what with landslides and snowslides, falling trees and rocks, and high winds and forest fires; the company keeps a man patrolling the line constantly to repair trouble and if possible to foresee and avert it. We call him the Trouble-Shooter, and he has to be strong and active, as well as brave, for the work is often dangerous.

"Long Pete was trouble-shooter on this line for years, and of course he had plenty of adventures. Oh no, *he* never told them; you could as easily get that dynamo to talk about itself, as Long Pete. But once or twice I happened to get in on something myself."

"I remember one awful hard winter, with sleet and snow till it seemed it would never stop. There are often wolves in the valley here. But they don't bother us, for I keep no live stock. But that year they went clear over the ridge into Bernard Valley and harried the farmers. Pete would often see them, and sometimes he would be trailed by them if he came back late, but he never got excited. 'Bunch o' varmints on the mountain' he would announce casually as we sat at supper after he had arrived in the evening.

"'Did they follow you?' I would ask, hoping to get a story."

"Yeah, a little," he'd say. And that would be the end of it. But I knew from past experience with the man that he had had some sort of a wild race or dangerous escapade, or he would never have mentioned the matter at all.

Well, he got started one morning out of Bernard with a hard trip in sight. It was snowing on the mountain as he could plainly see from below, and he had trail to break. It was just past noon when he reached the half-way cabin just this side of the top, and he stopped long enough to cook and eat a hasty meal. Then he got out his phone and hooked onto the line to call Bernard, but the line was dead. He tried Power house with the same result. It was clear there was trouble in both directions, and no way of knowing where he was needed worse, but he decided on this side, gathered his kit, and started. He always carried phone, block and tackle, and splicing wire, besides his tool kit, and it made a good load. He left his revolver at the cabin this trip to travel as light as possible, and started down the mountain going fast on skis wherever the way was clear.

But he found trouble soon enough. A lodge pine held him up for an hour of hard chopping and rope work. Then further down he had to dig the cables out of a drift in a deep gully and stretch them tighter to swing them clear. He phoned me to cut them out, one at a time as he worked, for it's dangerous business, working with a high-tension electric cable.

When he was through there and had phoned me to cut in the last one, he said he'd head back to the cabin next and make an early start for the other side in the morning.

Well, you know how a man will work at top speed under excitement without feeling tired, and then when it's all over how he'll let down all at once and be completely fagged out? It was that way with Long Pete. When he'd gathered his tools and was ready to start back he realized it was later than he'd thought, and he was tired enough to lie right down there in the snow and sleep. He decided then to come down the mountain and work his way back up next day. So he started again following the line down and counting towers as he passed them, for he knew Hanging Rock wasn't far away.

They didn't have the iron ladder down the face of the cliff in those days; you had to make a detour of a mile to a ravine where you could get down. Pete left his load under a tree close to the line and started for the ravine, but he took the block and tackle, for he thought he might need the rope to get down the cliff. It was growing dark when he struck the trail, and he hadn't gone far before he couldn't distinguish the trees any more.

A narrow strip of timber had been cut away along the brow of the cliff, and he was obliged to go carefully, steering by the grayish light that edged away into the black gulf overhanging the chasm. It was ticklish work, for at any moment he knew he might start a slide that would carry him over the edge, and he kept as close to the trees as possible. The instinctive fear of the cliff caused him to hug the timber and frequently he would find himself among the trees and be obliged to strike a match to get his bearings back. Feeling his way in this manner was slow, and after a long while he came to a place where he knew something was wrong; he had bumped into a tree, and striking another match, moved out as far as he judged safe, but he did not find the narrow clearing he expected. His match went out, but he slipped along a little farther in the darkness. The pine boughs brushed his face and he parted them to pass through, when suddenly he felt the snow slip away beneath his feet.

He gripped the mass of twigs with both hands and held on for dear life while the entire drift gave way and slid with a roar over the cliff and into the valley below. His skis went with the slide—it was all he could do to keep from following them—and a big cloud of snow flakes filled the air.

It's enough to scare the bravest man to have the ground fall away from under you that way in the dark, and when Pete had managed to crawl back along his bough to the tree he was weak. He hugged the trunk and tried to think. Gradually it dawned on him that he had passed over the head of the ravine, which must have drifted full, and had come back to the far edge of the cliff beyond the clearing. Disgust took the place of fright now, for he saw it was out of the question now to either get down here or back up to the cabin in the deep snow and darkness and without skis. He had counted strongly on sleeping in a good warm bed that night. He would have to camp till daylight came and he could fix up some sort of snowshoes. But he didn't intend to camp right on the edge of that cliff, with the danger of another snowslide starting at any time.

He decided to backtrack to the power line first, and striking another match, he located his earlier tracks and noted the general direction. Just as the match went out he heard, from somewhere on the mountain, a sharp, high-pitched howl that he knew only too well. There were wolves in the timber.

Right there is where I would have lost my head, but Long Pete was too good a woodsman for that. He started out, floundering in the deep snow but keeping to the trail by the aid of his matches,

He came to a clearing where he could see better, and was making fair progress when he heard the howl again. It was answered by another that seemed nearer, and soon after there was a sharp yapping which, he knew, meant that the wolves had struck trail. It might not be *his* trail, but he would have felt a good deal better if he had had his skis and a gun. Still he wasted no time in speculation but floundered on.

Whenever he paused near a tree he would pull a twig or two, and when he had a good bunch collected he applied a match to the clump of fat pine needles. As they blazed up he waved them to get a better light, and holding them above his head, looked back. A dark mass on the dimly-lighted snow told him all he wanted to know. The wolves *were* on his trail, and closer than he had supposed; but they had stopped at his light. Hastily, he made a bigger torch of more boughs, then started on, pausing every few yards to wave his light and yell. If he could stand them off till he got to the line clearing, and then keep his blaze going while he found his axe, he wasn't afraid of the result, for Long Pete had always held that Grey wolves are cowards and will not attack a man unless they have a clear advantage. Still he had never known them to come so close before; they surely must be famished.

Then Pete remembered that a pack of Black wolves had been reported in this region—the farmers over Bernard way had supposed they must have come down from Canada, for there were none native in these mountains. He had not paid any attention to the report, but the boldness of this pack alarmed him now. He paused to renew his light once more, and this time, as the flames leaped up again, a pair of greenish glowing eyes shone from the darkness of the timber close at hand. He yelled and leaped toward the beast, which slunk back. He glanced behind him—the rest of the pack had approached still closer. There was little time to lose now, and he knew it. Any stumble or show of fear would bring them instantly rushing in about his heels.

As he plunged forward he saw the line clearing ahead, and gathered himself for one last effort. But then he saw three dark forms leap from the shadows and place themselves boldly in the opening. He yelled and dashed at them, but they held their ground. His torch was flickering, for in his desperate rush he had had no time to gather fresh twigs. He was surrounded, and it was evident they would try and pull him down the instant he entered the open space, for those in the rear were closing in.

There was but one thing to do, and he did it mighty quickly. Hurling the glowing brand at the pack, he leaped for the branches of the nearest tree and drew himself up as the rush of the followers carried them beneath. It was a close call, and he did not stop climbing till he was well up in the tree.

The pack at once set up a yapping that would have given almost anyone the ague. Pete hung to his tree panting and perspiring till he had regained his breath somewhat and begun to get chilly. By that time the pack had settled down to watch and wait. It was a question how long he could stay on his perch, for it was awfully cold that night. Finally, just to be doing something, he began to break off boughs and throw them down at the brutes. He could see nothing below the tree of course, but out in the line clearing he could make out the forms and see them move as he tossed branches down.

He unhooked the block and tackle from his belt, removed a block and fastening it to the end of the rope, tried throwing that. As he was dragging it in after a few attempts, the hook caught and he pulled up a coil of splicing wire. He had not realized this tree was the very one under which he had left his tools. He was nearer the line than he had supposed. For a moment, he thought it might be possible to fish up the telephone and connect it in some manner to the line. But that, he reflected, would most probably end in his own electrocution, for in the darkness he would be as likely to hook a high tension cable as a telephone wire, even if he could throw the cable that far, which wasn't probable.

Then Long Pete had an inspiration. He might freeze to death in the tree before morning, but he would at least throw a scare into that wolf pack, or have some fun trying. He began to break away more boughs on the side nearest the clearing, till he could make out the high tension wires in the dim light. They were about at his own level though several yards away. He uncoiled the heavy wire and, bending one end into a hook, he securely tied the rope to it, with the pulley block still attached for weight. Then, clambering down to a lower branch, he gathered a big bunch of twigs, lighted them, and dropped the blazing mass.

As it lighted up the space below, the entire pack drew off into the clearing. He climbed back to his former perch. He could see the wolf pack grouped on the snow now directly beneath the line, and he steadied himself for the throw, coiling the slack rope loosely on his left arm. Then, hanging the coil on the stub of a torn off branch, he threw the block out with all his strength at the wires in the air.

As the rope uncoiled, the heavy wire trailed after it and, by great good fortune, the hook caught on one of the high tension cables. The free end of the wire swung down, landing squarely among the dark milling forms below. As it touched ground, there came a flash and a smell of burning hair. One wolf crumpled up on the snow; and the others leaped back snarling into the timber, as sparks continued to flash and sputter near their fallen companion.

Slowly, Pete drew the wire back upward a bit, handling the rope gingerly with his heavy mittens, and held it free of the ground till hunger and curiosity drew the animals back. They circled about the unmoving form, sniffing, until at last one laid hold of it with his teeth and began to back away. Then the rest leapt in, tearing and fighting over the carcass.

Pete tried to swing his wire down on them again, but by now they were too far away and too much occupied with their feast to run from the flashes. He waited. The dead wolf was dispatched in an incredibly short time, and the growling ceased as the beasts began to sniff about for stray bits. After a while he threw more branches under the line and dropped his wire into the pile, producing a display of fireworks that lighted up the whole clearing, and eventually burned his wire in two.

After another wait, he climbed down to the lower branches again and tossed a few more blazing twigs on the ground. No wolves were to be seen, so Pete descended calmly to collect his tools.

                                *   *   *

We were in bed when the phone rang, and somewhat surprised as you may imagine, to hear Long Pete's voice apologizing and asking calmly if we would bring him a pair of skis. "Better fetch your gun, too," he advised. That was all, but it was enough.

We started, the boy and I, with lanterns and guns, and when we got to the top of Hanging Rock, there was Long Pete, with his long-handled axe at his side, before a blazing camp fire, seated on a bunch of pine boughs as comfortable as you please.

It took me most of that long winter to get from him all the story of how he had been treed by them black wolves.

Rescuing Effie (ca. 1920)

By William S. Jennings

Marcia regarded her annual summer visit to Sister Effie's farm home as a sort of penitential pilgrimage—a concession, as it were, to the existing institutions of family relationship and country life, both very necessary to society in general, but entirely outside Marcia's personal requirements. And having appeased the gods of Duty and Conscience with a two-day penance at the farm, and the palate of three husky little farmers-to-be with wonderful boxes of candy, she was wont to kiss each sticky face dutifully and each furrowed one heartily, and settle herself on the 6:40 accommodation train for the city with a comfortable consciousness of virtue. Thenceforward her face was turned eagerly ahead to the possibility of flirtatious adventures for the rest of her vacation time.

At the Dawes School of Business Practice, Marcia was admittedly a drawing card. When she led a class things were sure to hum. "We always make it snappy," the principal would assure each interested visitor as they peered in at the door of the long room where a regiment of typewriters clattered madly away, and Marcia, smiling brightly, maneuvered the operation with the poise and finesse of a general. It was because of her poise, her smile, and the new business which they brought to Dawes School, that Marcia was so able to maintain her own flat, her vacation trip, and habiliments of the elite. The principle knew whose salaries he could afford to boost, and he did it—when he had to. Marcia saw to that.

The penitential visit had wasted one day. They were sitting in the gloom of the old side porch of the farmhouse watching the bobbing of a lantern where the men were finishing the milking at the barn. Sister Effie, stayless and expansive, in flowing faded gingham somewhat soiled, rocked heavily over the protesting floor boards. She regarded with admiration the French slippers and the exquisite silken calves of her sister perched in the high swing. In the pale glow of the oil lamp, she studied the smartly cut short skirt with its wide black and white stripes, the delicate fluff of pongee which subtly suggested alluring curves, and a vague discontent stirred in the farmer's wife. Effie herself had been just pleasantly plump in those romantic days when her cavalier used to drive up the lane of a Sunday evening, the white-ringed harness gleaming against the glossy black of his horse, his buggy spokes glistening in the glow of the setting sun. Effie had worn her own harness well in those days, too.

Glancing over, Marcia read Effie's wistful look, and understood it.

"Why don't you come to town with me, Ef," she suddenly blurted, "and buy yourself some nice things?"

Her elder sister started, then checked herself. What was the use?

"Where on earth would I ever wear 'em?" she parried wearily.

"Why right here, in the evenings if nothing else. The family would enjoy it. And Jim can certainly afford the cost."

"Oh, it ain't that. You wouldn't understand, Marce. Farm life just ain't that way. I used to think it ought to be. But it ain't."

Marcia could not see the overflowing eyes in her sister's shadowed face, but she caught the tremor in her voice as she said these words. It sounded as if Effie was overburdened—was on the point of breaking. The hopelessness of Effie's solitary task, of keeping up Jim's old ancestral home—built in a day when servants were plentiful and cheap—struck the younger sister forcibly. She hesitated, fearing to provoke an outburst of tears.

It was Effie who spoke first, having got her voice under control again.

"I'm just tired, I guess. I oughtn't to be. Lots of women around here do what I'm doing and live just this way, but . . . ."

"But you and I were raised different," Marcia objected. "Those women never knew anything else."

Just then, a distinct odor of fresh sweat, and a heavy step on the gravel walk preceded the arrival of Effie's husband from the barn. Jim sat down on the porch's bottom step.

"You girls talking secrets?" he inquired after a time.

"I was just telling Ef that she ought to get herself some nice clothes like she used to wear, Jim. She drags around here like a washerwoman."

"That's just what she is—a washerwoman. And I'm just a common laborer. What's the use of us trying to make out we're anything else?"

"No we ain't, Jim."

Effie's protest forestalled Marcia's sarcastic reply.

"It ain't that we don't care," Effie went on, "We just haven't time—with a table full of farm hands to feed and a houseful of children to rear a woman don't have any time for herself. And your work keeps you bustling every minute, too. And if we ever do get any free time, we're mostly too tired to enjoy it."

"Well, hard work's nothin' to be ashamed of, I reckon," insisted Jim. "Hard work is honorable, ain't it?"

"Of course it is," Marcia retorted. "But there's no reason you can't have a little pleasure along with it. Dressing up of an evening now and then, having nice things and going places. I don't see why farmers couldn't do that as well as other folks. It all helps."

"Bah! That's book farmin', Marce. Sounds all right in the newspapers, but you don't see real farmers livin' that way. Not in this whole county you can't name one family that does—not one!"

Marcia didn't try to answer, her acquaintance with real farmers being restricted, but her faith was strong. In her silence she resolved that somehow or other she would help Effie and the children to find something of what she termed higher life—let Jim stay dead among his clods if he would.

When she arose next morning, breakfast was almost ready, early as it was. Effie, wearing a stiffly clean wrapper now, and with neatly combed hair, was making coffee.

The men came in from the barn, washed together in a corner of the kitchen, splashing their faces and arms with cold water from the bucket, leaving the clean towel heavily streaked and the floor wet. The still smelled strongly of the cow stables and of perspiration as they took their places at the scarred oak table. Marcia declined their invitation to join them, saying she would eat later with her sister and the children, who were not yet awake. Effie waited on the men at table.

"Think you've got to go, do you Marce?" Jim's question had the stiff finality of polite disinterest in it.

"Oh, Jim, I've stayed longer than I ought to have stayed now. Think of all I've got to do!"

"Yeah. I'll bet your busy: no help nor nothin'." Jim winked slyly at his wife.

"Jim, you remember what we were talking about last night?" Marcia went on.

"Clothes wasn't it?" He grinned at the men around him. "I've never known it to fail." The men grinned back, nodding.

"You don't care for them at all I suppose?"

" Oh they're all right, Marce. But we ain't got no time for 'em here on the farm. It's just like Ef says."

"Look here, Jim. Don't you remember how pretty Ef used to look when you'd come driving up to our house on Sunday evenings, and slip me a bag of candy to keep me out of the way?"

"Oh Ef was a peach in her day, all right."

"You found time enough to dress yourself up too, in those days, and to keep your horse and buggy shining, didn't you?"

"We didn't have no kids then, Marce," Jim reminded her gravely.

"Anyway, you'd like to see her look as pretty now as she did then, wouldn't you?"

"Why sure. I'd give a thousand dollars. What're you trying to sell, fat reducer?"

Jim dodged an imaginary projectile from his wife's direction, and laughed heartily at his score.

"Look here, Jim, I want Effie to come up to the city all alone this fall and stay a week with me. If I promise to doll her up as fine as she used to be, will you promise to let her come?"

Jim's laughter died as he turned his head and caught the gleam of unexpected hope in his wife's eyes.

After a moment, he said "Sure. I ain't stoppin' her if she really wants it."

"Well, that'd be mighty nice," Effie sniffed, "But I'd like to know who'd take care of the children all that time."

"Oh that's easy enough," Marcia answered, efficiently. "We'll ask Cousin Sue to come over, and you can do something for her sometime. I tell you Ef, you women down here have just got to wake up. Talk about keeping the children on the farm! You folks have a poor way of making farm life attractive to them I must say!"

"I don't know's I want to keep them on the farm," confessed the mother.

"Well I do," asserted Jim. This farm's goin' to be a real money maker some day. I'm plannin' to buy the Baker forty this fall. But how will I manage then if the boys don't stay here and take hold when they grow up? I don't want you putting any foolishness in their heads neither," he warned his wife.

"They'll have minds of their own, Jim," Marcia prompted sweetly. "You can't drive folks nowadays—you have to lead them."

"Sumpin' to that," asserted one of the hired men. But Jim sat silent.

"Well, brother, what do you say? Is it a bargain?" Marcia asked, holding out a hand.

"Sure," Jim sighed. I said I'd let her come. I'll kick her out and lock the door behind her whenever you say you're ready."

Jim and Marcia shook hands gravely and the men all went out laughing.

Later, after a hasty breakfast while the children still slept, the two women drove together to the station.

"I'm not blaming you, Ef," said Marcia softly as they stood waiting for the train. "I think you're doing splendidly with those children and all the work. But it's too hard on you. I want to help you a little, that's all."

"Oh I know Marce, and I'll be glad to come. But you can't change things that way. It is a hard life we live here, and it's just as hard on Jim as it is on me. I really wish we could get away for good. I'd be willing to work at something in the city myself if Jim would ever agree. He could make as much money there and we could have some pleasure. But he'll never leave. He loves all this—our place, the land."

Effie sighed. "I used to think the country was pretty, but nowadays I can't see anything but the ugliness of it all. And I hate to see the boys grow up to the same life."

The train bell began to clang.

"Well Goodbye, I'll write you when I'm ready," Marcia said, and climbed aboard to be whisked back to the city and everything that made her life worth living.

Of course, just what that may include depends entirely on your point of view. To Marcia Peyton, two rooms and a kitchenette with a woman to sweep on Wednesdays represented the pinnacle of what life had to offer in the way of domesticity. And her apartment was located within easy walking distance of the shops and theatres—the acme of desire. A real house, with a garden and flowers, a loyal husband, three active chubby children, and quiet evenings spent sewing or reading by lamplight—in short the very things so satisfying to the mother heart of women like her sister—seemed to her mere necessary evils which those of her sex less fortunate than herself were obliged to endure in exchange for protection and board, a bargain she considered very poor indeed.

Yet she loved company and delighted, on occasion, to serve a full dinner herself to a few friends. But it was only as a relief to the monotony of solitude. Her guests came and went, but she might have been sexless so far as their occasionally professed adoration ever evoked any response in her heart.

Sister Effie, stepping from the train two months later, was not exactly one's idea of the typical country woman. Yet how should that type be described at a time when types are changing as rapidly as today? There was nothing about her which the most fastidious might have considered funny, yet she revealed in every move a certain lack of confidence and of ease which betrays the untraveled.

Sufficiently laced, Effie did not shake overmuch, and her ruddy complexion, toned down by a bit of talcum, might have been the envy of many women, and the excitement of adventure had already brightened her eyes. For the rest—brevity might have made her skirts more modish, yet Effie's ankles were no longer slim, and French heels were not designed for women of her heft. Her gray gown and broad hat were not bad. She was purposely coatless, for that want was to be supplied on the trip.

All this Marcia reviewed as she watched her sister descend the steps that led from the elevated tracks, and she became instantly eager with plans for the transformation. "If I don't tog her up to date now," said that young lady to herself, "then no one can. Jim and the boys are certainly in for one great big surprise when she gets home!" Little did Marcia know how much of a prophet she really was.

A few days later, two unattached gentlemen of Marcia's acquaintance learned by telephone that a small party was to take place at her flat. It was to be a theatre party with supper afterwards at the Vendome. They expressed delight with alacrity. One of them volunteered a motor, and suggested that the supper take place at his country club, adding that the moonlight should be especially fine. And thus it was arranged.

Sister Effie found the first part of the evening a bit difficult, even with Marcia's vivacious assistance. The certain knowledge that Marci's wizardry had by now made her decidedly attractive helped. But making conversation with a strange man was not easy for her. She kept comparing him to Jim, and could not be quite sure where the advantage lay. Effie was instinctively distrustful of soft palms and carefully manicured nails in a man. She tried not to think of what would happen to those slim tapered palms in Jim's horny grasp. The man's shoulders seemed to her ridiculously narrow, and his chest flat. She actually caught herself wondering whether that chest were grizzled with hair as a man's should be beneath his silk shirt and the unseen garments below that might even be pink.

And yet he wore these clothes with faultless grace and was the soul of courtesy. No rough jokes of the sort with which Jim sometimes made her blush in front of company. So she smilingly accepted his compliments and replied to his sallies of wit as best she could until the curtain rose.

It was years since Effie had been in a theater of any sort, and never before had she seen such a one as this. Her inability to follow the plot of the musical comedy distressed her at first, until, reassured by the obvious pleasure on the faces of her companions, she at last relaxed and simply let herself enjoy the music, lights and pretty gowns on stage. At one point, when the footlights revealed a chorus of shapely feminine legs in a background of fluffy things, she crimsoned and pretended sudden interest in her program. Nor did she join in the general laughter that greeted many of the jokes on stage. Yet on the whole she enjoyed the experience thoroughly and was sorry when the curtain finally dropped. She wished that Jim and the boys could see—well, maybe not this, but something nice!

Driving out into the country was better. There was the play to talk about now, and crops. And there were many others present in the supper room. Marcia chose for her from the menu with accomplished ease, and Effie enjoyed the delicate and unfamiliar flavors. There were liqueurs, too, with a sparkle and a snap much finer than any Effie had known taking the odd medicinal nip from the old family flask. She had really never cared much for spirits, though she liked to have some about, for colds and things, as her ancestors had always done.

It was a lively party that made its way at last to the open touring car and roared off down the road.

The night was warm and fine and the man at the wheel drove faster than was necessary. The splendid motor hummed and the small black pointer on the dashboard crept slowly around the dial with such persistence that at last even Marcia from the back seat uttered a protest. Effie meanwhile was silent, astounded, white. Never had she ridden at such speed before, and when they passed another vehicle she gasped and held on tight as they skidded briefly then regained the roadway. Up ahead a bridge loomed. The car seemed to lift itself into the air and hurl them at the structure, then skimmed over the boarded floor with scarcely a rumble.

But at the far end of the bridge a sweeping curve in the road ahead flashed into the headlights. The suddenly bewildered driver released the throttle, but at this speed taking the turn required precise judgment—judgment not confused by sparkling liqueurs.

The scream and immediately following crash awakened the family of Horace Mayhew, farmer, who lived near the turn. Soon after, he and his two pajama-clad sons came rushing down from the sleeping porch to help pull the unconscious form of a heavy woman from the wreck and carry her into the house. The other woman followed, able to walk, but quivering and sobbing.

They telephoned for a doctor, after which the two men, miraculously unhurt but helpless to assist the injured woman, went back to right the car and discovered that it was still able to move under its own power.

That night, Marcia, for the first time in her carefree life, learned the true meaning of prayer. The doctor looked grim when he arrived, and was only reassured toward dawn when Effie awoke and smiled. At the sight of that smile, Marcia rushed out into the garden to demonstrate with grateful tears that, after all, her heart was altogether feminine.

"She's got to lie still though, for some days," said the doctor several hours later. And then, as he was leaving, agreed to a serious request of Marcia's which was made with subdued mention of the Dawes School. "No, of course not," promised the doctor. "And the newspapers too. They'll be reasonable, I'm sure."

Something about the Horace Mayhew farmstead was different, Effie realized, when she finally recognized that she was not in a hospital, nor in her sister's city flat, but in a farm home. There was a soft rug covering the hardwood floor in the bedroom, and a few very interesting pictures hung on the wall. Through a door she caught glimpses of white tiling and enameled bathroom fixtures, and her eyes were eased by the soft glow of an electric light near the bedside, placed just right for reading if she cared to read.

But Effie had no need of reading. There were diversions enough during the days of her convalescence in her new friendship with the farmer's wife and family.

The windows were low and broad, and through one of these she could see out into the garden. Its long straight rows were very clean and thrifty and the young man who worked there frequently carried himself with a jaunty bearing which the invalid found most pleasing.

"I do believe that boy of mine would *live* in his garden if he could," said Mrs. Mayhew one day, noticing her patient's interest.

"Oh, is he your son? I s'posed he was visiting you. He doesn't look exactly like—well, like a farmer."

The mother laughed. "He has been away a lot. Six years at the university. Just finished this spring."

"Six years!?"

"Yep. Altogether."

"Is he going to teach or something?"

"Goodness no. Hal wouldn't think of anything but farming."

"But—six years!"

"Well, you see he took the regular university course for his degree, and then went to the agricultural college after that. His father says a farmer needs as good an education as anybody else. Our other boy's doing the same thing now. He has three years to go yet."

"Doesn't it cost an awful lot?" hazarded the invalid.

"Yes—but they're all we have, and we feel it's worth more'n the money to them, or us either. They have their own livestock here and all and they farm summers. They pay their own way, largely."

"I'd think you'd want them to settle in the city, or something, with such good educations."

"Oh, goodness!" Mrs. Mayhew's explosion was eloquent. "That's the last place I'd want my boys to settle. I was raised there. My father slaved at a desk till he died. Never knew the real meaning of health and freedom like you can have in the country. Farm life is such a sweet restful existence,"

Effie looked skeptical. "Well maybe, if you can *afford* to rest."

"Why, my dear you can't afford *not* to! At least I don't see how. That's what Horace said when he first started in to fix our house all over some fifteen years back. The boys were little then. They were plenty of work and not much help. 'Laura,' he says, 'you've got to take it easy's you can.' He said that to me when we debated whether we could afford the changes to the house. And it has been wonderful. I don't believe I could've stood the work all these years without it, and help so high now-a-days and hard to keep."

It was only when the patient was able to leave her bed that she fully came to understand the wonders of machinery that had so transformed the washerwoman of the Mayhew farm. She had to see the electric washing machine buzzing cheerily—doing the work of two women while its owner dried her dishes. The contribution of the vacuum cleaner to the immaculate house was another revelation. Likewise the water supply electrically pumped right indoors, the power churn, the mangle in the laundry and the fireless cooker and stove combined. They were all new and wonderful to the farm woman of Hobbs Station, and they all spelled rest and life to her. She understood now the secret of this wonderful dream home in the country, and she developed a great dread of returning to her own dreary surroundings.

Marcia, arriving one evening for her daily visit, received a distinct surprise. She had expected to find her sister up; but depression of spirits she did not expect. However, by tactful questioning and shrewd guessing she gradually discovered the source of the patient's distress.

"It's the boys, Marce," Effie confessed at last. "I've been thinking of them all day. If only things could be like this for them. But you know how we are."

It was then that a brand new chapter was added to the expanding conception of real life in Marcia's brain. And, as usual with Marcia, action followed close upon impulse.

Effie could go home on Friday, the doctor had told them. There were yet two days. It would be enough. She would have a telegram delivered to Hobbs Station. Telegrams were non-committal thing that stirred folks sharply and allowed no argument.

"How is she," was the first question from the brawny visitor who stopped at the door of the typewriting room in Dawes School on Friday afternoon.

"She's fine now, Jim, soothed the smiling young general, "but you'll have to wait and go out with me to see her. I'll soon be through. I'll explain everything as we go."

At the door of the Mayhew home they were met by Effie herself—sweet and smiling in the original Peyton way.

Jim looked in bewilderment from one sister to the other. "Marce," he began, "You durn little liar—" but his mouth was stopped by Effie in a very effective way. "Well you *are* a peach anyhow," he concluded, holding his wife at arm's length to get a good look at her.

He was right. This was a very different Effie from the one who had departed two weeks ago for a short visit that had been lengthened first on one pretext then another.

Effie was rested. She was reduced, a little, and her slight pallor was beautiful contrasted with the black organdy and lace of her new dress. Her hair was done as she used to wear it years ago, and altogether Effie seemed to have turned the clock back by about ten years.

"And now that you're here," she said, you're to stay to supper. Mrs. Mayhew won't excuse you. She told me so. Here she is."

Jim felt like a mouse in a strange garret. The three Mayhew men to whom he was introduced at supper were surely not farmers. They wore loose shirts with short sleeves and belted trousers, and the slippers on their feet could never have come near a hay field. Yet the men had been putting up hay all afternoon, and as far as he could understand it, their talk ran mostly on crop yields and machinery. Jim was hearing a new language—filled with terms like "crop residues," "soil analysis," and "acid correction." These and other equally strange words fell easily from the lips of the two young farmers, and their father seemed to have a real respect for the terms.

"Book farming," Jim thought to himself at first, and could not understand the elder Mayhew's tolerance of it. He could tell at a glance that the father at least was a real farmer, a practical man.

"You really think it pays," he queried as they smoked together out on the porch after the meal.

"Mr. Mayhew smiled in a quiet way and replied "I admit I didn't have much faith in it when we started. But their mother insisted we give it a try, and I'll tell you, friend, it doesn't do for an old man to be too cocksure of anything these days. Times are changing, and a lot of our old farming ways are plum outgrown."

"Why man," Mr Mayhew went on, "what can you do when they take hold of a field side by side with you and make it return two or three times as much as you can? You've *got* to admit it pays. Hundred bushel corn—fifty wheat! I tell you!"

"Yes, it pays all right. I'm sure I never could have cleared the mortgage doing things the old way. But we've done it, sure enough, and fixed the place up to boot. And now I'm takin' it easy and the boys are running things. Come have a look around!"

They walked together to the barn. On the way they passed a small, neat building made of concrete block. "Bath house," said the owner briefly. "Ever hear of a bath house on a farm when you were a boy?"

"Nothin' but the swimmin' hole," Jim grinned. "We had us one of them."

Inside the building were a row of showers, with a smooth concrete floor and a partitioned space at one side studded with hooks for hanging the light clean clothes the men had warn at the table.

"I guess I snorted some when they first mentioned this," the father admitted. "But as in most everything else, I finally gave in. Now I'm for it. It only takes a minute to slip out of your work clothes, kick off your shoes, jump under the shower, and grab a towel. Why the boys do it 'bout as fast as you'd wash up at the pump—and man how fine you feel after! I honestly believe the hired hands do more work now. Leastways nobody goes to table dirty and smelly no more. We all like it."

The clean, well-lighted dairy barn with electric milking machines was a revelation to Jim. He watched as the attendant moved rapidly from cow to cow adjusting the milking cups, and carrying back full pails of warm milk to the separator in an adjoining room.

"One man does all this?" Jim asked.

"Yep," replied his host. "Plus cools the cream from twenty cows and feeds the skim milk to the pigs while it's still warm."

"This dairy set up is another place the boys put one over on me. We had some cows I thought were fine. Good lookers they were. But the boys ran some tests and showed me the figures. Sure enough a lot of them cows weren't paying for their feed. Well, I had to give in. We beefed 'em, and replaced 'em, and the dairy's been putting us ahead ever since."

That walk was Jim's new birth—for at every point the talk turned on dollars—an argument the farmer from Hobbs Station could not controvert. And a host of new ideas, foreign as yet to his part of the state, came crowding into his consciousness.

The last straw was the mention of the farm engineer.

"What's that?" he asked in great humility.

"Well it's a feller who takes hold of your farm and plans it all over again—and darned if every item in his plan don't either make you money or save you labor, which amounts to the same thing. Oh sure, he charges. But your increased income will more than pay for him—far more. I might have worked all this out without him, but it would have taken me years instead of weeks."

It was late that night when their guests left the Mayhew farm. Effie, clinging to her husband's arm at the front gate was astonished at his final admonition to his host. "Now Mister, don't fail to shoot that farm engineer down to my place right away—before I change my mind."

And once they were settled on the train, she leaned contentedly against him.

"Jim," she asked innocently, "what ever is a 'farm engineer?'"

"Well, I guess you could say he's a man that figures how to make your farm work better."

"But won't he cost an awful lot, Jim."

"Not as much as the Baker forty would. And we need him a lot worse, Effie. Besides, it'll all come back to us—the money we spend on him."

She considered this for a moment, then smiled.

"That's just what we're doing, too, isn't it. Coming back."

"Back to Hobbs Station, you mean?"

"No-o, Jim. Back to life!"

Article by William Silver Jennings

[from *The Northern Herald* (Cody Wyoming) 30 September 1910]

Supt Jennings Discusses School Matters In Cody Opposes Free Books—Why

Superintendent Jennings of Cody's public schools today contributes an article that is worthy of the careful perusal of parents and citizens who are interested in the education of the children of this community. Mr. Jennings has promised *The Herald* to contribute, from time to time other matter from his pen.

———

Editor Herald:

We have always been a great admirer of the humble hen who goes quietly about the serious business of egg-laying and reserves her crowing until the job is finished and the goods delivered. It would seem that at that stage of the game she has earned the right to crow a little and might even be pardoned a feminine "I told you so." To one of quiet Quaker propensities it would seem that the best way to do anything is simply to begin. To omit the flourish of trumpets and the vociferous voicing of big predictions, and in the parlance of the back yard to "saw wood."

The teachers and pupils of Cody's schools have been for three weeks thus accumulating a supply of fuel and the superintendent feels like apologizing for having consented to do any talking at all. There is indeed little to talk about. The pupils and teachers are working as they should. Harmony is reigning as it should, with here and there a momentary overbubbling of youthful American pugnacity—a sign of healthful growth and life. There is nothing phenomenal about Cody's schools, a fact for which we congratulate ourselves. The world does not need educational phenomena—just healthy, normal conditions.

The enrollment is good but not perfect. Attendance in the grammar school is 177. In the high school 38. There are pupils who should be in school but aren't. It is hoped they will not long remain outside the fold.

The most conspicuous weakness of our school system, it seems to me, is one which we cannot avoid for the reason that it is fastened upon us by the law of the State. I refer to the free textbook system. Doubtless there are many parents who are glad to be relieved of the necessity of purchasing school books for their children, and yet just why the state should undertake to furnish free school books any more than free school shoes or slates or jumpers and pinafores, except in cases of real inability to pay on the part of the parents, it is hard to say.

It is certain that the system is open to serious objections from the educational standpoint.

In the first place it is a well established fact that gratuitous distribution of any commodity lessens the individual's regard for the commodity. Public charities have long ago found out that it is better for the individual to pay something for what he receives than to receive it without effort. The rule holds here. Children do not hold free textbooks in the same esteem as their own private property. The fact that father's taxes contribute to the purchase of the book does not figure strongly in the child's mind. The book is not his. It is public property. As a direct result he is not so careful of the book. The first result of the system is that pupils are given a lesson in the careless use of books. A most pernicious lesson.

It is well enough to say "let the teacher teach them to care for the books." The teacher can do police duty over pupils and books if necessary, but it is too bad that the state should *make* it necessary. And after the policing is performed and the books preserved, the damage is still extant in the character of the child—the lack-esteem for his book, and the loss of the sense of responsibility that comes from private ownership.

Another evil in this connection lies in the very manifest injustice to the child of placing before him a second-hand book which another fellow, or half a dozen others, have soiled and saying to him in effect, "keep this clean and nice." He knows the fellow who used it before did not keep it clean, and as a matter of fact he *could not* keep it clean if he used it properly. For be it known that school books are made to be used, not preserved in glass cases.

The boy who really knows his book will have it dog-eared and marginal-noted. It will have made numerous trips home and back again with him and been his companion in many queer places. It will be *his* book and he will be as familiar with all its oddities and niceties as he is with the habits of his little dog. Fancy an active boy using a book thus and keeping it perfectly clean. As well expect an industrious carpenter to keep the paint unscarred on his new axe.

A third evil is this unsanitary and unpleasing feature: distributing to a roomful of clean and happy children an armful of dirty second hand books—germ-inhabited and uninviting.

The thoughtful parent who is solicitous about his child's welfare will surely prefer to spend a few dollars and supply his child with new books that will be his own private property. His to work with and live with and learn to love, and finally to put away carefully on dusty shelves whence occasionally in the years to come he will take them down and fondle them and leaf them through and live again the lively scenes of his schoolboy days.

The free book system may be all right commercially and politically, but it is pernicious from the ethical and educational standpoint.

—W.S. Jennings, Cody, Wyoming

ROBERT KIMMEL JENNINGS

Born 1912 in Cody, Wyoming, raised, after his father's death by a maiden aunt, attended Purdue University, earned a Master's Degree in bacteriology, came east to work in a lab near Philadelphia, where he met Edith Eaton (a Quaker by convincement) and married her in 1940. Four years later, their son Lane was born. Moving to Chicago in 1950, Robert worked full time at the Rheumatic Fever Research Institute, while earning his PhD from Northwestern University. He later became a civilian scientist for the Office of Naval Research, stationed first to San Francisco then to Washington, D.C. eventually retiring from the post of Head of the Biochemistry Branch of ONR in 1980. Long addicted to poetry, Robert wrote poems and stories for a number of local magazines in the late 1940s, and, after his retirement, joined the Iona Poets group in Washington, DC, remaining an active member until his death in 1996.

Poems by Robert Kimmel Jennings

FRIENDS' MEETING (ca. 1948)

No granite signpost indicates the sky
As though to say, "This way to God above!"
For here they hold the All-Pervading Love
Need not be sought afar, but found close by.
A sylvan setting, soothing to the eye,
The harmony of oriole and dove,
Designs laid on by ivy's lacy glove—
These are the arts by which the Quakers try
To lure the soul away from sordid things.
And, in the meditations silence brings,
They strive to banish from them for a space
The urgent interests of life's troubled race.
Then, when more strident voices all depart,
God's gentle whisper sounds within the heart.

ISLES OF THE BLEST (ca. 1988)

When I was young, I doted on
A velvet, evanescent fawn
Who came to me, when chance allowed,
And led me to a rainbow cloud
To drift across a dreamy bay
To pleasant islands, far away,
To laugh and dance in ecstasy
Beneath a Monkey-puzzle tree.

But that was very long ago:
My fawn must be an aging doe;
The acid rain have blighted, quite,
The magic isles of our delight;
The airy boat that bore us there
Have foundered in the jet-torn air;
And learned apes with high degrees
Have solved all Monkey-puzzle trees.

For they have solemnly decreed
A flower, untended, is a weed;
All rocks must crumble; clocks run down.
All eagles tumble; goldfish drown;
They never see a rising sun
Or fertile fields where floods have run;
Their butterflies incite the breeze
To level Monkey-puzzle trees.

But now I view, with joy (and fear),
Another childhood drawing near
And dream—perchance it draws along
Another joyous, gentle fawn
To guide us to a new-born shore
Where apes and aircraft are no more;
Where we may breathe a blessed breeze
Blowing through Angel's-Answer trees.

KINDEST WISHES (ca. 1945)

I wish you well, my little son—I do indeed.

I wish you work too difficult to ever know
The weary bones of boredom. I wish you wages
Low enough, at first, to learn the greater recompense
Of work accomplished, quite apart
From any sense of earning.

I wish you trials
Enough to find the hidden ally
Of your heart and mind.
I wish you pride:
The humble pride of teamwork
With the least and best.
I wish you hearty pleasure,
Singing courage, utter rest.

God grant me wisdom not to curb
Your lust to handle life,
Nor weaken your heart's greatness
By protecting you from strife.
I wish you well, my little son.
I do, I do indeed.
I wish you may become a man—
A man whom all men need.

THE JUDGMENT SEAT (1940s)

This man's black, and that man yellow,
The other man is white:
Where's the man that has no color
To say which color's right?

This man labors, that man ponders,
The other rules the earth—
Where's the man, to none beholden,
To say what each is worth?

This man weeps, and that man hungers,
The other fears the night.
Let him who never knew a burden
Tell whose cross is light.

IN HIS OWN IMAGE (undated, 1940s?)

From points and energy and mind,
God makes the Universe and Space.
With paths of points and lines of time
With rays of light—the Will Divine
Creates His mansions (made for Man)
Within this many-mysteried place.

From God-wrought substance, Man creates
Pyramids and molecules—
Transient marvels, small and great;
Wheels and steels and swords and tools.
God makes the clay; Man molds the clod
And mansions styled "The House of God."

Those miracles which underlie
Creations we can comprehend
Evade the human touch and eye:
We miss the message they imply!
WE deal with clay and stone and sand,
And fancy "God is like to Man!"

THREE DOUBLE DACTYLS[1] (ca. 1990)

SPELL

DOUBLE!, you Dactyls! You
Sonorous syllables!
Pat-a-cake, pat-a-cake!
Find me a word!

Something not utterly
Incomprehensible,
Libelous, nasty, or
Wholly absurd!

[1] The double-dactyl is a verse form supposedly invented by the American poet Anthony Hecht and Paul Pascal, though earlier examples are known to exist. For more background and examples of this addictive form consult <*http://en.wikipedia.org/wiki/ Double dactyl*>.

PLACEBO[2]

Higglety-Pigglety—
Hermes, Thrice Marvelous,
Treated Egyptians (I
Find this is odd),

Selling them soluble
Abracadabaras,
Taken in cocktails. They
Made him a god!

[2] "Long before penicillin or specialists, sick Egyptians were given magic verses written on papyrus, ground up and stirred into wine. It all began with Hermes Trismegistus, incarnation of the Ibis-headed god, Thoth. And to this day, physicians vie for recognition as 'The Doctor (i.e., Learned One),' with the big bill."—R.K.J.

BIRD-LOVER'S REVERIE

Rat-a-tat, rat-a-tat
Erythrocephalus
(Red-headed woodpecker)
On my tin roof:

What if you puncture it
Quasi-intentionally—
Where will that get you, you
Rattle-brained Goof?

THE DODO (1993)

Now the Dodo's over!
(Dodo's day is done.)
Settlers and Sailors
Slaughtered him for fun!

Dumpy, dawdling Dodo!
Hungry Human Sinners!!
Mingled (in the Islands)
At dandy Dodo dinners!

Come the resurrection
Who will rise again?—
Harmless, hapless Dodo?
Or those *horrid* men?

INSPIRED VERSES (1987)

A Guide for Beginners

Shakespeare succeeded in print, stage, and screen
Having won favor with sad **Melpomene**.
Applause is delivered with bravo's, *con brio*
Because he was blessed by historical **Clio**.
We delight in his drama—his verses, also:
He was dearly beloved by sweet **Erato**.
Yet this finest of poets would be but a twerp
Had he not been devoted to tuneful **Euterpe**.

You claim you don't *care* about fame? What a liar!
(For stardom, apply to—and bribe—**Urania**.)
You'll get the applause that you're hankering for
If you dance attendance upon **Terpsichore**.
If you pray for the favor of **Polyhymnia**
You may find your words set the whole world on fire!
Should humor inspire you, most readers will hail ya
And laugh at your jokes—thanks to bucolic **Thalia**.

So struggle, young poet, and don't give up hope:
You may be Teacher's Pet of the Glib **Calliope**.

[**NOTE**: The names in bold are those of the 9 Muses who dwelt on Mount Olympus and served to inspire devotees of the various arts. The *pronunciation* of these names however is my father's own invention, and owes more to poetic convenience than to the laws of Greek grammar.—LEJ]

FISHING (1988)

An inverted honor guard
of poplar, aspen, birch,
marches into oblivion below us
as we, silently, drift shoreward—
a mustard seed of meaning
in a universe of undecipherable intent.

Drift with the olive-drab cork.
Let no paddle endanger
the saran-wrap trampoline
that carries us betwixt
the sunset-gloried cathedral above
and the tree-haunted infinity below.
Let only the loon risk that!

THE FETISH (ca. 1948)

A watch—still running! Shirt, and shoes, and hat.
A suit, with signs of wear about the hem.
A billfold: money, photos, such as that.
Some keys. A pipe, with teethmarks on the stem.
A body too, of course—but what's *it* worth?
It's broken now, and quite beyond repair,
A cold, unfeeling lump of nascent earth;
But on it we will lavish all our care.
He moved, and loved, and sang, and wept. And talked
Of beauty seen and intimately known.
The laughter in his eyes, the way he walked—
These were the things we loved as his alone.
In truth, this hat he molded with his brow
Holds more of *him* than what we'll bury now.

HAVING LEFT TOO SOON (1988)

Now and again I find it
Rather pleasant
To rouse my father, briefly, and
Astound him with

Automobiles and telephones
Which have no cranks;
A furnace without ashes;
A horseless city.

He would, however, gladly trade
The White Marsh Shopping Mall
For three clumps of cattail
And a red-winged blackbird.

IKEY (1992)

In the bottom drawer
Of my father's desk
Lay a neat, pen-written,
Ribbon-bound
Bundle of letters,
Each signed "Ikey."

In an attic trunk,
Lay the ivory pen
That wrote them.
Beside it, another
Bundle of letters
Also ribbon-bound.

These were in envelopes,
Each addressed
To Miss Irene Kimmel
But each one beginning
"Dear Ikey," and the authors
Were many.

Before this visit
Into my parents' past
I would have said
Language serves best
To make facts clearer.
But does it, really?

The name "Irene Kimmel"
Served the mailman
Well enough. But love
Began
When the calm aloof woman, Irene
Emerged as "Ikey."

SPIRIT OF SEVENTY-SIX* (1988)

Now you break trail
For me a little while:
The blizzard blowing
Has risen to a gale—
Frozen my smile,
But not yet stopped my going.

*We braved the spicewood-fragrant
Fern-entangled Sandy Bank
Together, you and I,
And, when the moss-oiled boulders
Were too slick for chubby legs
You crossed the minnow-haven torrent
Safely on my shoulders.*

Thus, I was a giant once, all wise,
Waking wonder-worship in your eyes.
You owe me nothing.

*Together, we squared up against
The Paython and the Zulu and Burmese,
Dueled Aramis and Long John Silver,
Sniped with the Martins and the Coys,
Stretching a little then—
You forward and I, back:*

Our hearts met midway—
We were of an age.
You owe me nothing.

You strode through Cambridge and Hong Kong
While I, more slowly, threaded labyrinths
Of Golden Gate and Washington
A world apart, yet side by side.

> Shoulder to shoulder, sharing pride
> One in the other, then as now
> > You owe me nothing.

Stand beside my rocker.
Run my errands. Bring me
Holmes, dinosaurs,
And your good verse
Without my asking
That we still may share.

> You owe me nothing . . .
> But break trail for me
> A little longer,
> As only you know how.
> Childless, you in your turn
> Are the giant, now.

*[dated 16 March, when RKJ had just turned 76 years old]

Stories by Robert Kimmel Jennings

Why The Loon Laughs (1948)

By Robert K. Jennings

In the lovely land of the Northern Lakes
Lives the Loon, a curious bird, who makes
A noise that sounds like silly laughter
(Which he would NOT do, if he didn't haughter!)

The Loon is a queer sort of duck. He is rather handsome, and could be a very pleasant bird if he just wouldn't laugh like that all the time. It isn't the sort of laughter that is laughed at something funny, you know. It is a mad, sad sort of laughter, as if the joke were on the Loon.

Besides laughing, the Loon swims and dives in the cold Northern Lakes. He is very good at it. When the quiet of evening comes to the North Woods, and the bright moonlight makes the silvery underside of leaves twinkle like jewels when the wind blows, it is fun to watch the Loon sailing gracefully about on the lake, diving here, and coming up unexpectedly some place else. If he just wouldn't make that silly noise all the time!

I don't think you'd care to be a Loon,
And swim at night by the light of the moon.
But I'd be willing to bet my hat
That you'd like to know what he's laughing at!

It was this way. A long time ago, when birds first came into the world, the Eagle was made Emperor of all the birds on earth. It was his job to see that rules were made and obeyed, to make speeches on grand occasions, and to be sure that the sick and needy birds were taken care of by those better off. Being Emperor is a mighty big job.

The world is too big a place for one bird to rule it all by himself. The Eagle couldn't settle a squabble between the Cuckoos and the Cockatoos in China, *plus* help lay a cornerstone for a new Martin-house in Montana the same day. So the first thing the Eagle did after he became Emperor was to travel all around from one country to another, appointing other birds to be Kings to rule when he wasn't there.

> *The birds were excited as anything*
> *When they heard he was coming to choose a King,*
> *And each tried to outdo the rest*
> *In finding a way to please him best.*

The Swallow planned to dance for the amusement of the Imperial Eagle. The Hummingbird was going to show him all the loveliest flowers in the North Woods. The Owl wrote a very long, very wise speech. And the Loon decided to give the Eagle a finer present than any Emperor had ever had before. He wouldn't tell anyone what the present was to be, except one old Frog who was his pal.

> *The Swallow was going to put on a dance,*
> *But it seemed pretty certain he hadn't a chance*
> *To impress his Majesty more than the Loon*
> *Who fully intended to give him . . . the Moon!*

"Can't do it! Can't do it!" said the Frog.

"You think the moon's too high up, don't you?" the Loon replied. "Well, that one is. I've flown very high indeed, and the moon is always higher. But if you can keep a secret, I'll tell you where there is *another* moon just like that one. The fish have it, in the Lake! I've often seen it on nights that are still and clear enough, shining deep in the water! I'll dive for that one."

"Won't work! Won't work! Too DEEP!" warned the Frog.

"I can dive clear to the bottom," boasted the Loon, "and it can't be any deeper than that!"

> *"Just think, Mr. Frog," said the Loon in glee,*
> *"What a wonderful present it's going to be!*

With his own private moon to light the way,
He can travel by night as well as by day."

"Won't work!" the Frog insisted.

The day finally arrived, and the birds all gathered to welcome the Eagle to the North Woods. The Owl gave a very long, very wise speech in his honor. The Eagle listened politely, but was seen to cover his beak with his wing a time or two. Then the Swallow darted into the sky and swooped and swayed and did all sorts of dancing tricks. The Eagle applauded him, but said nothing. And then the hummingbird led the Emperor to all the loveliest blossoms in the woods, for which the Emperor thanked him—but nothing more.

Meanwhile, the Loon had hurried out onto the lake to the spot where he had last seen the Fishes' Moon. Down, down he dove—past the Sunfish and the Perch, past the Pickerel and the Pike, and finally past the Dogfish which slouches along among the weeds at the very bottom of the lake. But he couldn't find the moon!

"Tolja so! Tolja so!" chortled the Frog, who was watching from a floating log.

"They've moved it!" decided the Loon. "I'll find it yet!" So he commenced swimming about the lake, diving here and diving there. Every time he came up without the moon the Frog gloated, "Tolja so!"

Some folks say that the Loon's mind, which was never too good anyway, began to crack a little right then. And it may be so,

For he asked the Sunfish, he asked the Perch,
But neither would help him in his search.
After all, when the Fishes' Moon one wishes
To steal, he is loony to ask the fishes!

The Loon hated to give up, but along about sundown the Eagle called all the birds together to hear an announcement.

My fine feathered friends," he began, "you have all done your best to make me welcome, and I am very grateful. The Owl showed great wisdom, and the Swallow was very agile, and the Hummingbird led me to a great deal of beauty. These were nice things to do. But one of you, in a humble practical way, did something even kinder and more thoughtful."

For a moment the Loon had a wild hope that somehow he had succeeded after all. The Eagle continued.

"The Fisher bird, alone, realized that I might be hungry after my trip, and quietly brought me a fine, sweet Sunfish to eat. Other birds may be wiser, more graceful, or have a finer sense of beauty, but the simple kindness the Fisher displayed shows that he is best suited to be your King. I take great pleasure in fixing this crest upon his head, by which you may all know that he is your King Fisher!"

All day long on the Lake the Loon
Had passed up Sunfish and hunted the Moon,
For it wasn't the Sunfish that he had been after—
And so he broke out with his sad, mad laughter.

The Loon still thinks if he could find that moon the Eagle might change his mind. You will still see him hunting and laughing and diving all about the lake. And the Frog is still insisting, "Won't work!"

Two Chapters from

The Emerald Tablets (Ca. 1966)

(an unfinished novel)

By Robert K. Jennings

[**Synopsis**: A traveler seeking wisdom comes to the Temple of Thoth which also houses the laboratory of the legendary alchemist Hermes Trismegistus. He poses his questions both to the priests of Thoth [clergymen] and to the adepts of Hermes [i.e., scientists] and from each he receives answers that appear mysterious—until he recognizes that they are saying the same thing in different languages. The priests use parables and the scientists use mathematical formulas. The two stories presented here contrast the true natures of heaven and hell.]

With Great Sagacity

Pilgrim: In the Outer Court, the Priest speaks of the Law, and promises reward in Heaven unto him who obeys the Law. Is this a vain promise?

Adept: Hermes has this to day: "With great sagacity, it doth ascend gently from earth to heaven."

Pilgrim: How shall I learn what Hermes wished to communicate by these words?

Adept: The temple gardens, as you will have observed, are of great beauty. This is due to the skill, the labor, and the wisdom of the gardener. Many there are who find that the gardener can plant seeds of thought as well as seeds of flowers. It may be that he can help you.

*   *   *

"I don't know why you'd come to *me* for advice," said the gardener, sitting back on his heels, "though lots of people do. I can't say why they think I can help them, seeing as those inside the temple have got all the learning I never had a chance at. Still, folks do come—neighbors and friends, sometimes even strangers like yourself.

'*Sam*,' they say, '*I'm miserable because I can't have so and so*'—that's the young ones, mostly—or, '*How am I going to make out now that such-and-such has been taken from me?,*' that's more what the older folks want to know.

All I can ever tell them is what I would do, and that's generally what I have done myself at one time or another. I've wanted things I couldn't have, needed things and done without, just as much as the next man, though I can't complain."

"What were you," asked the Pilgrim, "before you became gardener here at the temple?"

"Not much of anything, or whatever I had to be to get along, I guess you would say. My parents died years ago when I was just a baby, and Old Missus over there on the garden bench, she took me in and did for me until I could help myself some. Old Missus never had very much for herself, but she never begrudged what she did have and never looked for anything back for what she gave. Of course, as soon as I was old enough to see that, I tried what I could do to pay her back for what she done for me."

"He was always a big help," the old woman chimed in pleasantly. "Even as a tiny bit of a boy, he helped me in the house and did chores. Did them for other folks too, later on, to bring us in a little money. Sam always was a real hard worker and a good child to me that had none of my own."

"Old Missus gave me a good home, and we've been real lucky and have it still. Lately she's been poorly and can't do much for herself, so I don't like to leave her all alone. She'll come down here with me to the temple and sit here keeping me company while I work. It's a real comfort to have her here where I used to be all alone so much."

"Sam *would* say that. He don't tell you he has to carry me here and carry me home, nor that he'd get his work done a whole lot quicker if he didn't have to stop and fix for me all the time. Most folks I know would complain and try to find some way out, but Sam's not like that. It's like he's found contentment somehow. Maybe that's why folks seek him out when they want advice."

"Seems to me," said Sam, "finding ways to get out of work is lots harder than doing it as a general rule. Work makes you tired, true, but it also makes you strong so you don't get tired so soon. You can be sad about getting tired, or you can be glad about getting stronger.

You take old Josh, used to live down the road a piece from our cottage. Got himself a son-in-law who was a good enough boy, but puny. Josh didn't have no patience with weakness and clumsiness; he preferred doing all the work on the farm himself, and Cecil let him do it. That is until Josh fell off the roof he was patching and got himself pretty badly busted up. Then things changed. Old Josh hated it worse than sin being laid up and having to let his family take care of him, but it couldn't be helped.

'Sam,' Josh said to me, 'Cecil here means to help all he can, but he just ain't used to hard work and he can't do it. But if it don't get done, how are we going to eat? What'll I do? I can't stand just lying here, but I can't get up neither.'

All I could say was what I would do. 'Let him *try*,' I said. 'He won't do as good a job as you did, but if he tries he'll do something,'

It was sure hard on Josh to see things not being done right—not the way he'd have done 'em himself. But Cecil did get better at it as he went along, and he got stronger, too. They went through some real hard times, them folks, but they come through it, and now that Josh is gone, Cecil's every bit as good as Josh himself was. Which he *wouldn't* of been if Josh had kept on doing all the work right up to the end."

"Sam," said Old Missus, "I wonder could you get me a drink of water? I hate to trouble you, but I'm mighty dry."

"Let *me* get it for you," offered the Pilgrim.

"You don't know where to go, and it won't take me but a minute," Sam insisted. "You just keep an eye on Old Missus for me while I'm away, and I'll be obliged to you."

As Sam disappeared among the trees, Old Missus turned to the Pilgrim.

"Sam really don't mind doing things like this, and I wanted a chance to say some things Sam maybe wouldn't want me to say."

"He's a real angel on earth, Sam is. You have no idea how hard a job it is to do for me these days. I can't hardly lift a hand, and he can't leave me so he either takes me along or he don't go. Some folks would be miserable, you know, trapped like that. But I purely believe it's what makes Sam happy.

I know for a fact it's what makes folks admire him and look up to him, which they wouldn't do if had just himself to take care of."

"In a way," said the Pilgrim thoughtfully, "your troubles give him importance, don't they? Thanks to you, he is needed and depended upon. If you were better off, he would be worse off."

"Well now, you might say so. Of course Sam wouldn't think of it that way. Profiting by my misery isn't something he would want to do. I wouldn't want him to know that I ever had such a thought, and don't you go telling him!"

"I must be hard for you though, having to let Sam be strong and well and get all the credit too."

Old Missus sighed. "I did used to feel kinda sorry for myself." She admitted. "But then I got to thinkin' here's Sam: he's strong and he's kind, and folks look at him and say what a fine man he is. It is true he can do the work he enjoys doing, which I can't, *and* get praised for doing it. But if it weren't for me, he couldn't. Where he has pleasure in his work, I have pain that makes that work for him—that's something *I*'ve given *him* don't you see?"

"Sam is like a well full of good water," she went on. "It isn't worth a thing unless there's a cup to put the water in, and then it's worth a lot. Well, I'm that cup. So I'm worth just as much as the well, as helpless as I am."

"But doesn't it bother you that Sam gets all the credit?"

"It did. Like I said, he get's paid and I get pain. But I got to thinking, what good is praise after all? If folks think you're worth more than you are, it's a sham and don't mean nothing. And if you really *are* worth all they think you are, then it won't much matter to you that they know and think it too."

Old Missus took the Pilgrim by the hand.

"Sam's every bit as good as folks think he is, and it ain't too much to say he's maybe worth more than even they guess. But the fact is, I'm doing a bigger and harder job than he is, only don't you ever let on I told you that!"

Things Superior and Things Inferior

Adept: And now, having considered the Heaven that has been promised as a reward for good works, you will no doubt wish to know if there is, in fact, also a Hell as the priests have warned. Hear then this story of one practitioner of the Hermetic art in its darker form.

————————

Professor Herman Dreigrosschen taught ancient Greek at Beanblossom College in Indiana. The student body of that modest institution was drawn from places as distant as the farthest corner of Morgan County, and numbered in its heyday some two hundred and fifty young men of humble origin and still humbler means. Even judged by the academic standards of the 1920's, the faculty at Beanblossom was not well paid. To Professor Dreigrosschen, at that period in his career, a winter overcoat with three intact, functioning buttons would have represented a significant upgrade.

It is not exactly clear why the Professor refrained from flunking Hezekiah Smith, since the boy could scarcely read more Greek by the end of term than he had at the beginning—which was none at all. Yet it is known that he did not do so, a circumstance for which Hezekiah was grateful. He expressed his gratitude to the Professor by making him a present of a book, handwritten in Greek (possibly the incentive that had led H. Smith to sign up for this particular course in the first place), a book which he assured the Professor had been handed down in the Smith family for many generations.

The book, purporting to be inscribed by the great alchemist Hermes Trismegistus himself—though obviously a forgery in this respect, since its leaves were clearly fashioned of rag paper, not papyrus—proved to be a late medieval grimoire or book of spells. It its preface, the author warned that dire consequences to the reader might result from attempting some of the more potent spells contained within. In particular the author stressed that any bargain made with the Devil would most certainly result in eternal damnation. However, it failed to make Hell seem less attractive than the Chair of Ancient Languages at Beanblossom College, nor the accommodations to be expected there any more uncomfortable than those of the ten-dollar-a month attic room which the Professor now occupied in Widow Malken's ramshackle house on the outskirts of town.

Furthermore, the Professor did not believe in the existence of the Devil anyway. From his point of view, a man like himself might easily benefit from closer examination of such a book, and most certainly could have nothing to lose, since he did not believe in the existence of his immortal soul, either.

Still, the Professor was a bit upset, a few nights later, when the Devil did indeed appear as advertised inside the pentagram which he had carefully chalked on the bare floorboards of his meager rented room. It certainly caused him to give additional, if belated, thought to those introductory warnings.

Not, of course, that he was ready to forego this new-found opportunity for self-improvement. He was merely impelled to take a few precautions that he might have otherwise neglected. Thus, he shrewdly employed two of the three wishes the Devil offered him to minimize any likelihood that he would ever have to keep his own side of their bargain.

As his first wish, Professor Dreigrosschen demanded permanent association with a Familiar of some convenient type who could and would obey his every command. The Devil very properly demurred at this, pointing out that it constituted an evasion of the intent implied in granting only three wishes in the first place. The Professor shrugged and told the Devil that was his price, take it or leave it. The Devil fumed and stamped a bit, inside the pentagram, but at last, reluctantly, agreed.

It occurred to the Professor that the more unpleasant aspects of his bargain might be avoided if his own death were to be postponed indefinitely. He therefore demanded immortality in the flesh as his second benefit. He recognized his error when he caught the gleam of triumph in the Devil's eye, and noted the alacrity with which this particular wish was granted.

Thus warned, his third wish was for absolute immunity from any form of physical suffering, systemic malfunction, or infirmity. At this the Devil flew into a great rage, granted the wish with a snarl, and disappeared with a resounding crash which brought Mrs. Malken racing upstairs to the Professor's room in a towering fury.

When the landlady had been dealt with, if not pacified, the Professor sought relaxation in a quiet smoke. He reached into his pocket for his tobacco pouch and pipe.

However, he was startled to find instead a large grey mouse. His first instinct was to recall Mrs. Malken and return to her some of the same irate and unflattering verbiage which she had left echoing in his own ears. Two considerations impelled him to alter this intent however. In the first place he remembered just in time that his rent, though nominal, was still, as of that moment, three months in arrears. Secondly, it occurred to him that this mouse might be his promised Familiar. To test this hypothesis, he cupped the mouse in his palm and whispered, "See here, Mouse! Bring me a billion dollars in gold."

Considering that the experiment was not well planned, it proved to be extremely enlightening. Not only did it demonstrate immediately the financial advantage conferred by his bargain with the Devil, it also vividly illustrated the effectiveness of his other two precautionary demands. The Professor, though undamaged and feeling no constraint or pain, was, of course, now located at the bottom end of a huge golden piston which had plunged downward with great force through all three floors of the poorly constructed house, smashing timber, furniture, and the unfortunate Mrs. Malken on its way.

As no damage had been done to the exterior of the house, it was several days before anyone learned that the Malken residence was now a hollow shell, and its recent owner a particularly unattractive corpse amid the debris within. The Professor was not found; and there was no obvious explanation as to what had taken place, since the Professor had at once sent the gold back where it came from and obtained in its stead a modest billfold containing one valid example of each legal denomination, which, when spent, was instantly replaced by another just like it. Though rumors were rife in Beanblossom, no satisfactory answer to "the Malken mystery" was ever found.

The excitement had not yet died completely down when the Professor suddenly reappeared in town at the wheel of a new Stutz Bearcat, followed by a chauffeur driving a Rolls, with its back seat piled high with boxes of silk shirts, expensive shoes, and warm three-button overcoats. This small parade created a sensation in Beanblossom, Indiana, and it must be said that some uncharitable souls viewed the sudden acquisition of so many worldly goods by the academician with considerable suspicion—especially in light of the unexplained goings on at his former domicile. So strong was this feeling, in fact, that the College administration felt called upon to demand Professor Dreigrosschen's resignation.

This he granted without argument and without rancor. He then proceeded to buy the college campus lock stock and barrel, immediately razed its buildings, and erected on the site a mansion containing over a hundred rooms. Naturally, this also led to comment.

But, by the end of the decade, few people remembered the humble origins of Beanblossom's leading citizen. No one marveled any longer at his seemingly endless string of acquisitions. By then it had been amply demonstrated that Dreigrosschen was an enormously wealthy man, and why should anyone be surprised if such a man chose to indulge expensive whims.

There was, however, over the years, a certain amount of gossip and conjecture concerning the number and variety of visitors who came as guests to the massive mansion. It was noted, for example, that Dreigrosschen's early associations with local merchants, stock brokers, politicians and the like diminished over time, and that an ever-increasing number of his visitors were female. At first, the ladies in question were all quite lovely, elegantly dressed, and obviously delighted to be there. Later arrivals appeared to be much younger and somewhat ill at ease. A few of these promptly left in a huff, while others were never seen to leave at all. There was even speculation in some quarters, that all might not be proceeding on a high moral plane inside the Mansion. But no one cared to make rash accusations without concrete evidence to back them up.

But a day came when evidence did indeed appear. The bodies of a young lady, known to have been a recent guest of the ex-professor, together with that of her fiancé, were found rather carelessly flung into trashcans out back directly behind the mansion. The authorities were compelled to take action, confident however that the Professor would have a perfectly reasonable explanation to account for this damaging circumstantial evidence. To everyone's surprise, he offered no defense of any kind, not even when he was put on trial, convicted, and sentenced to death in the electric chair.

This sentence had been carried out three times before the State of Indiana concluded that there was little point in continuing to install new power plants after the old ones were burnt out by overloading; and that, while Dreigrosschen might have sinned, he had been duly tried before the law and his sentence diligently and repeatedly carried out to a point where his debt to society must be considered paid. Justice having thus been served, Dreigrosschen was released and returned once more to his Beanblossom mansion, moody and depressed.

Workmen were called in, and the grand ballroom in the mansion was remodeled. The polished ebony flooring was torn up and replaced with equally polished Vermont granite. Into this was inlaid a ten-foot wide pentagram fashioned of large blue-white diamonds. Within the pentagram a kind of dais, made of fire-brick and cushioned with asbestos pillows was erected. Then the workmen were dismissed.

Once they were gone, the Professor took the grimoire from its vault and once again performed the prescribed incantations.

"How very thoughtful," said the Devil, observing the provisions which had been made for his entertainment. "I take it this means that things are going nicely for you these days."

"Well, no—not exactly," Dreigrosschen confessed. "In fact, that's what I wanted to talk to you about. Things are not going well at all."

"I'm sorry to hear that," the Devil assured him. "Has the mouse been giving you any trouble? I could give you a cat instead if you'd prefer it."

"No, no—the mouse does everything I ask. It isn't that."

"Then what does seem to be the difficulty," asked the Devil.

"Well, it's a little hard to explain. How can I say it? Look here, I remember once, before all this happened, I let a newsboy keep the change from a nickel when I bought a three-cent paper. At the time that nickel was the last one I had, and so the two cent tip was forty percent of my entire fortune. If I bought that paper today—even if I gave the boy a million dollars—I wouldn't be giving as much as I did then. Do you understand?"

"Mmmmm," agreed the Devil, "I can see that money isn't worth much to you these days."

"That's only part of it. I made this bargain to get something of value from it, and money isn't all that's worthless now. Suppose I bet this house on one toss of the dice? If I lose, I can welsh on the bet without penalty, or just have another house built. Suppose I fall in love and want to be loved in return; I can order my mouse to make it so, or I can wait and see if it happens spontaneously. But then if it doesn't happen, and I really *care*, I just have to wish and it happens after all. So even *reality* doesn't truly matter. There is no love for me to win, no money I can earn, no gift I can give, no risk to take, no thrill to experience—nothing!"

The Devil nodded sympathetically. "I can see just what a fix you're in." He shook his head. "It's *Hell*, isn't it?"

Article by Robert Kimmel Jennings

BIOLOGY—the Science in Man's Future

By Robert K. Jennings,
Head, Bio-Chemistry Branch, Office of Naval Research
[Published in *BioScience*, July 1966, pp. 37-38]

In the scientific mind there is a penitentiary wherein are incarcerated certain ideas which stand convicted of teleology, sophistry, or lacking visible means of support. We acknowledge the existence of these outcasts, but do not employ them, nor grant them voting privileges. Inevitably in such an institution, there must be a few individuals who are innocent of anything worse than being old and undefended. In the mental hoosegow, these notions are the clichés. They are facts which have seen better days.

One such concept is that of the biosphere. Biologists, if pressed may acknowledge that the world supports but one living organism, spherical in shape, highly differentiated, but demonstrably one entity. It displays a metabolism which we express in terms of carbon, oxygen, and food cycles. It has tissues, such as the hydrosphere, which is really a physiological fluid carrying nutrients to living elements suspended within it and removing their wastes. And the biosphere has organs, one of which is Man. We know all of this, but find it trite and not particularly relevant to zoology, botany, biochemistry, or politics.

The proper study of the biologist is the biosphere. But the title "Biologist" requires a bit of re-examination. Not too long ago each of us knew exactly what was meant by microbiology, by genetics, by physics, and by chemistry. Today, microbiology serves, and is served by, genetics. Genetics is a facet of physiology. Physiology has ramifications in electronics, which is an aspect of molecular physics among other things. Molecular physics is biophysics, and biophysics is biochemistry. Biochemistry and microbiology are inextricably intertwined, and we are back where we began. We have circumnavigated yet another sphere—the *sophosphere.* The sciences—physics, chemistry, biology and so on—are no longer areas of cognizance. They have become points of view, vantage points on the sophosphere from which to consider the world of energy and matter and life.

In this age of specialization, the Biologist is probably an allegory like Uncle Sam. Compiling the cumulative knowledge gleaned from many disciplines is a formidable task. But the tools and techniques of all science are available to biology as they are to all of the other points of view, and the capabilities for information storage and retrieval are growing along with the rest of the sophosphere. Perhaps it is not fatuous to speak of the biologist of the future in an allegorical sense, and it is certainly convenient to do so.

To what shall he direct his attention? In the tradition of the past, conquest of disease comes to mind. Cancer and heart disease are under attack and it is easy to predict victory. Victory bringing what? An increase of 2 or 3 years in the average life expectancy? Is this an achievement commensurate with the potential—and cost—of a sophospheric biology? What if all disease is eliminated? Where would that get us?

The possibility conjures up the mental image of a son struggling to support his aged father, his senile grandfather, and several vegetative great-grandparents. Is this the final goal?

No one can quarrel with the alleviation of suffering as a worthwhile objective. But, taken by itself, it is nearsighted. It reflects an implied scientific ethic which is, in itself, another cliché which has somehow never become indigent—that the proper study of Mankind is Man. We tend to take our dominion over the beasts of the field and the fish of the sea very seriously. It is our birthright and our reason for being. When science graduated from the selfish interest of the alchemist, the welfare of mankind became the standard of right and wrong. What has been done in biology and in physics and chemistry and in all the other disciplines has been considered important to the degree that it serves the human race. Burn the fossil fuel more cleverly for the profit of Man; pave the earth to make his passage easier; kill the pests which may annoy him; never mind what else may suffer: Man is all important.

This may be all very well if Man is indeed a collection of discrete individuals (as must be the case—unless the biosphere is something more than just a trite and smart-alecky cliché). But if Man is the organ of a larger organism, his welfare may not be best served after all by catering to his wishes and needs and comfort to the exclusion of all else.

Viewed in this light, concern about pollution of air and water, field and stream, becomes a larger matter than the philosophical sorrow of the ichthyologist for the tribulations of the trout, or of the ornithologist for the whooping crane. It has to do with the health of the whole dynamic creature of which we are a part. We need to ask whether a given technology harms the biosphere, not just how well it feeds or clothes human beings. We must learn quickly and accurately what the healing capacity of the biosphere really is and what constitutes a serious trauma before we decide to go ahead with schemes which appear justified if we accept that the object of all the universe is to produce, promote, and preserve human flesh.

This does not mean that we cannot seek to cure disease nor feed the people. It does mean that someone should weigh the consequences on a new scale of values commensurate with our present and future knowledge. The welfare of mankind can serve the biosphere as well, if homeostasis is preserved. Science can advance, and the provision of a logical goal should make that advancement more direct and measurable.

In such a scientific society, it would still be possible and desirable, for example, to establish comprehension of what chemical and physical events constitute learning. When and if this occurs, teaching should cease to be an empirical art since the teacher would know what it was he was trying to do to his pupil.

It may be pointed out that war itself is an ancient and established teaching device—probably the least effective and certainly one of the most costly of those which have been tried. If we knew what mind is, and what changing a man's mind requires, we should be able to use many more logical and economical methods to bring this about. And, in so doing, many innocent bystanders, human and otherwise, might be spared.

Such a capability is conceivable, and therefore possible. How would it be employed, and who would apply it? We have seen the various "teaching devices" developed by those who have considered matter and energy from their vantage points on the sophosphere. We have seen gunpowder and the atom applied by men who very honestly believed that they were serving the best interests of Mankind and that no higher aim was possible.

It would be nice, at this point, to predict what the role of the biologist will be in tomorrow's world. But all that can be done in fact is to call attention to what it *might* be. It is not likely that anyone but the biologically oriented will lead in an effort to establish wiser and more realistic goals for science and society than we have had in the past. And yet we seem to look forward only to disaster unless those goals can somehow be changed from the uncontrolled hypertrophy of the human race to the establishment of Man in his proper place in a secure and pleasant ecological niche within a healthy and balanced biosphere.

—Robert K. Jennings, Washington, D.C.

LANE EATON JENNINGS

Born 1944, in Wilmington, Delaware, but grew up mostly in and near Chicago. After high school, he attended Williams College, spent the summer after graduation teaching English in Hong Kong, followed by a year in Munich Germany as a Fulbright Scholar. He went on to Harvard where he earned his PhD in German Literature in 1970. That same year he married Margaret Ann Stone and moved to Washington, D.C., working first for the State Department, then for a trade association, and in 1976 became a writer/editor for the World Future Society, where he is still employed. After his first marriage ended, Lane married Cheryl Laughery in October 1987. A poet since high school days, Lane has kept on writing and translating, and, in 1992, became facilitator for the Iona Poets group. He lives in Columbia, Maryland, and has lately become an avid (if still novice) student of Japanese language, history and culture.

Poems by Lane Eaton Jennings

TO HIS COOL MISTRESS (1973)

"The times are bad, and people have no taste!" *
Catullus groaned; but added, on the sly:
"Let's go to bed—before we go to waste!"

I said: *"The thunder rolled when we embraced!"*
You said: *"It's just that dreadful lemon pie."*
See? Times are bad. Some people have no taste.

Tyrants grow careless, fall, and are replaced.
Where lovers make their beds they often . . . lie.
Still, let's to bed—before we go to waste.

A whisper never needs to be erased;
But words on walls deserve a smart reply
Like: *"Times are bad!"* or *"People have no taste!"*

Rubies are glass, and diamonds only paste.
The rich learn late: we *are* the things we buy.
Come quick to bed—before we go to waste!

Why argue? Facts are facts, and must be faced.
Boys will be...dead. Girls too. So don't be shy.
Since times are bad, and people have no taste,
Let's go to bed—before we go to waste.

* *"o saeclum insapiens et infacetum."*—Catullus, *Carmen 43*

ATHENS AFTER DARK (1966)

The bottle spoke only Greek,
but the wine
was easy to translate.
The waiter's yawn
was international—
contagious too.

Kiki, the dark-eyed siren
at my corner table,
had charmed the final
dollar from my shoe.

Bowing, I kissed her hand
and wished her
many rich Americans.
"Night-night,"
she giggled, wearily.
It was so late.

Winding back
to my hotel,
the town
lay heaped around me.
Lights were out on the Acropolis.
The fluted columns
hid their scars.

Streets gleamed
where the water trucks
had passed. And somewhere,
very close at hand,
a pair of lovers
I could hear
were laughing
quite distinctly
in my language.

CUPID WITH SPEAR GUN (1966)

What made us dive together
into that sunlit bay?
Our friends
were all away
and we were only
names to one another.

Side by side we swam
until my hand
collided startlingly
with your shoulder
spilling you, breathless,
into my arms.

Then, while the waves
danced out around us,
anyone could see
our opening smiles.
But no one saw.
Unless

that rascal Cupid
spied us from below:
our skins aglow, but
not from sunburn,
our approaching lips
already wet with tears.

REVIEWING MOUNTAINS (1984)

We never met again. What more's to say?
Deep country nights, we laughed
along white roads,
amazed by moonlight;
then danced apart.

Cities and days
reshaped us; but these hills—
green shadow and deep-running
stone—hold what we were.

Clouds lift this morning
over valleys cold as glass.
In rain-fresh roads
wheel ruts hold broken
mirrors for the sky.
Each step dislodges moss.
Pale birch and maple
tremble at my touch.

My eyes
could steal a fortune
from the wealth
of gold and greenbacks
sunlight scatters
on the forest floor.

Instead, they close
and squander all
on one lost girl
so many years away:

still wearing moonlight,
slim as a weathered stone,
bright as the bluejay's
morning chatter,
more truly April
than the wind
that plays the daffodils.

We never
met again.

What more's to say?

NOT UNGRATEFUL (1975)

Look at that moon, the bloated wretch,
grinning on high, while we
peer up like fishes
from the planty deep.

No beacon either, just a broken
mirror, scattering a little
of the true light back—
crumbs out of loaves.

But friendlier for that:
easy to fix on, and
draw near to. Sun,
you gave us everything;

We know, and we don't
mean to be ungrateful;
it's just hard to love
a light that burns our eyes.

From THE FOUR SEASONS OF LI HO* (1975)

UNBECOMING VERSE

Li Ho, the Litterer, rode out one day
scribbling hastily
and letting fly.
A painted bird flashed by.
The poet's old attendant,
following on foot behind,
blinded a moment by the startling wings,
let one small scrap
escape his eye
and float gently,
       unnoticed,
          to ground.

Entirely by chance
Li Ho, the Litterer,
did not ride by again.
Unclaimed, his composition
decomposed. Articulate worms
ran through it. Rain
poured over it. And sun and moon
by turns shed light
on doubtful passages.

Till finally,
old Editor Earth
accepted it (in altered form)
for his revised anthology
The Spring.

*The ancient Chinese poet Li Ho (T'ang Dynasty, 791-817) did exactly this.
[To learn more, look him up online under the name "Li He"]

OMAR KHAYYAM AND THE VOYAGER PROBES (1980)

Into the deep, machines—all systems
dancing on a needle's point—make voyage.
Where crystal spheres once sang,
now swarm the frequencies antennas ring to.
Robotic organs swivel, focus,
freeze, perceive new surfaces.
Ice deserts, canyons and peaks of stone, all
turn to points of phosphor
on a scanning-screen—to yes/no answers
in an endless catalog of queries.
Sounds become colors; colors turn to sound:
the solid sky reveals its contours
to the masters of the Calculus.

Flat on his back, Omar
observes the galaxy
extend her open arms.
He rubs his eyes,
befuddled by delight.
A desert wind sighs low
among the date palms: *Time*
    is a spider web of stars;
    and Man its starry spider.
Omar laughs to hear this,
but he writes it down.

Toward dawn, clouds overrun the sky.
Omar can't see his stars now,
and the sand is thirsty.
Signals degrade; the dancing masters
shake their heads. Objects remain
inscrutable—just out of sight, just
out of earshot, just
a glow beneath the skin.

Omar's asleep now. Does he dream?
Somewhere, beyond all clouds,
the systems whirl.

LATE HARVEST (1984)

Follow in silence
the winding trail
your ancestors' loaded wagons carved.
Slumped logs and drifts of granite
trouble your way. Step gently—
they belong here now.

Stand in a field
your ancestors cleared,
hipdeep in brown October ferns.
To these, you are winter-come-early.
Mow them down, rake them back,
stake out your claim.

Dig into earth
your ancestors turned—
through leafy mold
and roots as tough as wire—
decade by decade down,
one trowelfull at a time.

Harvest the crop
your ancestors planted
seasons ago—before
scrub pine and poplar rose up
choking the pasture
to its low stone walls.

Take up the treasures
your ancestors tossed aside:
whittlemarked bottles,
porcelain shards,
curious knobs of rusted iron.

Keep one or two;
the rest fold back
under the cradling soil
to gleam for younger eyes
in the light of another morning.

SHAKESPEAREAN BRAG (ca. 1986)

"Astronomers calculate that the sun
will explode in six billion years,
and destroy the earth."
                    —from a 20th century news report

At the end of Everafter, when our Sun
Gone feverish, swells up and sweeps aside
All we have ever touched, or held, or done
In one relentless incandescent tide,

The rocks will melt, and all the seas boil dry;
Trees smolder down to charcoal where they stand.
Glass deserts, mirroring an airless sky,
Will ebb and flow across the wasted land.

Poets of old, who guessed, but never *knew*
How Earth must end, promised eternal fame
To those they swore they loved—as I love you.
I know too much to match their empty claim.

But, treasured on board each lifeship
        fleeing out through Space,
Your image, Lady . . . (and my Art),
        will share a place.

OWL-GLASS (1987)

This autumn day an azure dome
crowns nature's
harlequin cathedral.
Life's waning
beckons everywhere
from feathery cloud
to leaf-deep forest floor.

Within his hollow oak, the owl,
that predator-poet, searcher-out
of mice and midnight wisdom,
wakes,
     blinks,
            questions
why a sun-gleam
angles at him
from the glass
some would-be birder
propped on a handy branch
to lure him into light.

But owl,
mellow with sleep,
and prone to sentiment,
mistakenly infers
some passing angel,
bored with reflected bliss,
let fall this mirror,
and flew off to die
if possible alone,
and muttering: "*To hell
with love! To bloody
HELL with love!*"

MOONRISE ON I-95 (1978)

Sun melts and runs across the west.
Dusk breaks, and the scrub woods,
where the asphalt ends,
come alive with wolves and Indians.

My headlights nip at shadows.
Hidden in leaves, barn owls and rabbits
flex for their evening run.

My tires thump the time
from underpass to underpass.
Speeders whiz by—so many
summer gnats.

Radio voices warn
of earthquakes and
recession, higher prices
if I fail to buy, of
death by cancer. I
believe them all.

What shall it be then:
suicide or murder?
Murder, this time,
I decide,
and silence my annoyers
with a twist of the dial.

So.
I am still the god
of my machines.

Now, in full dark,
I skim the neon bridge.
White glow, as of a distant
shopping center,
warms the far horizon.

Moon makes it new.

STARS (2000)

Imagine night
Without them:
Measureless dark
Forever unrelieved.

Who could believe
In purpose
Then; or make a wish
For anything but dawn?

Without stars,
Fire and lightning—
Ravening, brief—would be
Life's natural metaphors.

Sunlight erases
Every possibility but one;
Swaddling us
In a blanket of watery blue.

Add a moon, and still
The never-ending
Round of change
Affords small comfort.

Beyond our powers
To count or name,
Points that challenge us
To draw connections,

Scattered across
The roof all nations share,
The common field
Of every upturned eye,

Bridges of light
Our folly cannot burn,
Glowing gems
That never waken greed,

Clock of caravans,
Mariner's guide,
Smile-bringers no one
Can tax, or steal;

Stars
Are all the proof we need
That some things worth creating
Do survive.

FOR A CLERGYMAN AT 90 (2008)

I know a man who
Loves the *Word*
As if it were a woman
Or a dog
. . . *No,*
That's not right.

I know a man who
Loves the World
. . . *That's*
Not it either, really.

I know a man
Who *uses* Words
To *praise* the World
For all
He finds to *love* there:

Animals, seasons,
Children, the old,
All those in need
Of aid or comfort,
Ordinary ones
To be admired,
Moments worth
Treasuring.

And, by his praising,
Praises too
The Author of it all,
Who will, in time,
Reward him greatly,
In His perfect way,

As I do now,
Imperfectly,
A little,
In this song.

CREATURE COMFORTS (2005)

All through my father's funeral
a cricket chirped unseen.

Out on the lawn
as friends raised
parting toasts, a silent
butterfly clung near,
just long enough to hear,
then rose.

Suppose true ghosts
Assume no human form,
but come
as ordinary sounds,
familiar objects newly known,
appear
not often or for long,
but where they feel at home.

Some say
cursed places raise
eye-echoes
of resentments once removed.

Then joy,
tranquility, delight,
might equally survive—
raise revenants
that charm, not frighten:
birds 'round a feeder,
crickets on the lawn,
a single
          silent
                butterfly.

SEPTEMBER, 1996

for RKJ, who died 13 August

The month he never lived to see
Was one he would have loved—
Warm sunny days, cool nights
Tranquil with stars.

Birds flocked and jostled
At his feeder
Cats stretched and basked
Upon his windowsill

Deer nibbled fearlessly
Upon the tender roses
Strew in heaps
About the fresh-laid stone.

How he would have smiled!

Stories

by Lane Eaton Jennings

Busy (2008)

Busy afternoon in the bustling shop: coffee clatter, conversations, customers waiting in line, cheerful intense activity.

I'm lucky to have found this table—right by the wall but far enough away from an electric outlet that I feel no pang of guilt when someone carrying a laptop turns a hopeful eye in my direction.

I am writing with a pencil, old-style, out of the last century. A cigarette between my lips, or forked between the fingers of my non-writing hand, would fit the moment perfectly—but not the times. No smokers here. I haven't lighted up in thirty years; would probably just cough if I tried it now.

Instead, I concentrate on putting words around a feeling; scratching symbols for those sounds that have the power to make a human being magically appear in someone's mind.

Idly, I glance up, toward the door. I'm not expecting anyone; but . . . .

There she is. I see her. She sees me. Surprise turns to delight.

She passes effortlessly through the crowd, eyes bright and smiling.

I rise slowly from the table, grip its edge a little for support, welcome her in my turn, with eyes and smile.

We stand for just a moment facing one another; her hands clasped in front of her, mine at my sides.

Then, together, both of us bow, very deeply.

Sagesse Oblige (2010)

Wisdom is a woman. We are good friends. Plato would be proud of me.

I speak to her in long and complicated sentences. She answers simply, shortly, rarely. What can I say? She holds the cards. So long as I continue to amuse her, she is mine (at least in theory). Once I begin to bore her, she will go her way, and I will be back where I was before we met—not lost, exactly, just not headed anywhere worth being if I got there.

Sometimes I ask myself, how did this happen? Given the difference in our ages (does she age at all?) what could I possibly possess that she might find intriguing? Well, maybe candor. So many have come courting her—or claimed to do so—while in fact they really wanted one of her three sisters: Money, Power, Fame—someone to change them into something they were not before—make them the men they felt they *ought* to be.

I asked for nothing from her. That caught her attention, surely. I was content to learn, and in exchange I offered simple interest. She could be herself, just that; and I was genuinely happy to be in her presence, to observe, to listen, and occasionally comment or respond to what she asked of me, or offered for my own improvement. That must have been a novelty for her!

Imagine her at home, growing up, becoming who she is today, emerging like a flower from the snow. Who was the first to recognize her true potential? Some family member? Neighbor? Playmate? Teacher? Was she taught at all, or did she spring into existence fully-grown as some have claimed? Frankly, I doubt it. One thing I've learned from watching her behavior, not simply taking in her words, is that she makes mistakes—just never the same one twice.

Without mistakes, how could we ever know success from failure, ordinary from remarkable, easy from hard? Take languages. Hers is almost impossible to speak if you were not born into it. Yet sometimes it can be every bit as clear as any formal logic or mathematics. Most of the time though, it relies on hints and innuendo. Silence plays a large part, too. And so does knowing in advance who is worth speaking to, and why. Clearly it's not the things I say to her in her own tongue that draw her close to me, or keep her near.

Words in *my* tongue then? Yes, that must be part of it. I have some fluency, which seems to fascinate her now and then. But I credit the language itself for much of this. There are a thousand years of stylistic models I can imitate, still more if I extend myself and draw from languages I haven't mastered but can get along in well enough to ponder certain concepts outside monolingual norms—take for example terms like "*Weltschmerz*," "*noblesse oblige*," or "*mono no aware*." Wisdom is curious, you see; and never quite content with what she knows already. *More* is what she lives for. And, sometimes, I give her more.

How will it end? The two of us locked in embrace somewhere outside of time? I'd like that. But would she? More likely I will simply drop away, while she goes on—sadder perhaps for losing me, but more herself than ever for the various thoughts I've added to her store. And isn't this the final, most important, thing we all desire—to be both memorable *and* remembered?

*Cras Amet** (2011)

Cupid, aged 60, sagging, gray, stands atop a February hill, as he has done on this day every year for centuries, and conjures:

> *Cras amet qui numquam amavit,*
> > *quique amavit, cras amet.*
> (May tomorrow bring love to the loveless,
> > and to lovers—love renewed.)

It's a big job. These days, he thinks, perhaps too big. He wishes he were home in bed. And he knows exactly whom he wishes were in bed beside him. Psyche. Then he remembers. She was human, and she is gone.

Cupid gets back to business:

> Miraculous spring! Spring of melody,
> season of lovers united and courting birds,
> when trees, locked in the wind's embrace,
> shake out their hair like laughing girls.
> > *May tomorrow bring love to the loveless,*
> > *and to lovers—love renewed!*

Nothing happens.

The snow does not melt. The trees do not blossom. The birds are not singing. That chill wind blowing past his ear might actually be laughing—at him!

Cupit grits his teeth; conjures again:

> The land is alive with desire!
> The countryside thrills to the power of Venus.
> Even Cupid, her son, say the poets,
> was born in the springtime,
> and nursed on the nectar of flowers.
>> *May tomorrow bring love to the loveless,*
>> *and to lovers—love renewed!*

Still nothing. Nada. Zip.

Cupid shakes his head. That was then; this is now, he thinks. Its ages since I suckled anything remotely like a flower. I can't even remember what "nectar of flowers" tastes like. I was a baby, playing with my little bow and arrows. It's no wonder I was always getting into trouble. What self-respecting deity hands a loaded weapon to a child?

It's a good thing even we immortals age; only not as fast as humans. Zeus and the rest gave up, retired early. But I was just hitting my stride when the Roman Empire went down. Then came the Middle Ages! And the Renaissance! Chivalry! Romance! Those were the days!

Cupid bucks up; smiles; goes back to conjuring:

> See, Cupid lays his bow aside.
> He comes to dance among the nymphs,
> and not to do them harm.
> Ah, but beware, nymphs,
> for Cupid is handsome—
> even naked, he is not unarmed!
>> *May tomorrow bring love to the loveless,*
>> *and to lovers—love renewed!*

Any change? Perhaps. Still, not the awesome transformation he'd been counting on.

Cupid sighs. "*Even naked he is not unarmed . . .*" What a joke! Try that today, he thinks, and those errant "nymphs" would hot foot it to the authorities, have me hauled off as a flasher, a pervert! Whatever happened to innocent enjoyment? Careless rapture?

But wait. Is that a flower I see? Yes! Definitely. A snowdrop. And the air has changed too. It's stirring, restless, eager even . . . but still cold, still winter. Must try again.

Cupid shuts his eyes, clenches his fists in concentration, conjures:

> Bulls mount their heifers in the fields,
> and rams their ewes. The trumpeting
> of swans disturbs the quiet lake.
> The nightingale's lament might almost
> be a song of love—so sweet it sounds.
> > *May tomorrow bring love to the loveless,*
> > *and to lovers—love renewed!*

Cupid opens his eyes. Looks around, relaxes somewhat.

Better, still not perfect.

High overhead, a wedge of geese goes honking by, headed northward. Green shoots show here and there in the softening drifts. And, he thinks with satisfaction, if that yellow haze among the trees over there isn't buds about to blossom, I'm no judge!

Cupid smiles. With arms spread wide, he conjures one more time:

> When nightingales are singing,
> it is time for poets to be still.
> My muse is silent now. Apollo scorns me.
> But perhaps tomorrow . . .
> > *"Cras amet qui numquam amavit,*
> > *quique amavit, cras amet."*
> May tomorrow bring love to the loveless,
> > and to lovers—love renewed!

His eyes survey the landscape hopefully. Patches of bare ground here and there. A few extensive puddles. A clump of daffodils. Forsythia not quite open. Lots of mud.

Cupid shrugs. Well, that'll have to do. I had my doubts last year, but this time there's no mistake. Guess I just can't do it like I used to.

"Pssssssssst."

"Who's there?"

"It's me, the East Wind."

"*Eurus?*"

"The same. Heard you were out here blowing up a storm; thought I should tell you you're wasting your time."

"I am?"

"Yep. Climate change. World's turning in a new direction. Trust me, I get around. I know what's happening."

"What you really mean is I'm worn out. Finished!"

"No, no, no. Just listen, will you. Hem, hem. **Go East, Old Man!"**

"What's that supposed to mean? And what's so funny"

"Sorry, it's just that I've been waiting centuries to use that line! But seriously. All you really need is a change of venue. I know a place where you would fit right in."

"You do?"

"Oh yeah. Trust me. They need you there big time! Men. Women. Everyone. All they ever do is work, work, work. But you can make them happy. I mean *really* happy!

"I can?"

"Why not? You did it here for centuries."

"But I was young then. Just a kid . . . ."

"Okay. So it didn't stick! So what? People get older. Tastes change. What's cute at six, provocative at 16, can grow a little—how do I put this—"tired" at sixty. Take a good look at yourself."

"What's wrong with how I look?"

"Well, for one thing, you're naked."

"Oh."

"Right. Let's just say you'd like the way you look much better with clothes on. Oh, and another thing. Your name."

"What about it."

"*Dan Cupid*? Really? Definitely lacks tone for a distinguished older gent like you."

"Maybe you're right. Well, how about "*Romantic Love*, Esquire?""

"Mmmm. Okay. A little long perhaps, but better. Never mind. Out East they'll change it anyway. But not to worry, you'll pick up the lingo right away. Just find someone you'd like to practice with and . . . keep practicing! Got to blow now. 'Bye!"

[The East Wind exits, laughing.]

*   *   *

Sure enough, Cupid got dressed, changed his name, searched out that distant Eastern land, and made his home there.

Which is why, oh best-belovéd, should you ever travel to the island of Japan, you will find that Spring begins in February there; that Love (if not *too* brazenly displayed) is deemed appropriate at any age; and Santa Claus comes bearing valentines.

---

* Cupid's conjuration here is patterned on the *Pervigilium Veneris*, an anonymous Latin poem of the 3rd Century A.D. or later. Curious readers can find the original text, together with an English prose translation in the Loeb Classical Library volume on **Catullus, Tibullus, etc**. (Harvard U. Press, revised ed.1962 pp. 343-367).

Article by Lane E. Jennings

The Future Starts Yesterday*

Preserving Temporal Diversity and Other Futures for the Past

By Lane Jennings, Research Director World Future Society

[Expanded from an article first published in *Foresight Innovation and Strategy: Toward a Wiser Future*, Cynthia Wagner, ed., Bethesda, MD: 2005, pp 409-419.]

It is a common misconception that the past must be behind us for the future to begin. Idealistic young people and would-be political reformers in many times and places have yearned to "wipe the slate clean" and make a brand new start that would quickly lead society to permanent perfection. Sadly, history records that such attempts at sudden drastic change more often bring disappointment and sometimes disaster.

The pharaoh Akhenaton tried it first. Around 1360 BCE, he abandoned politics-as-usual, rejected war, freed artists to record exactly what they saw, and posited one abstract universal deity to replace the many special-interest gods and goddesses of Egyptian tradition. At one stroke, this revolution-from-above broke the power of the army, undermined the established priesthood, and changed the pharaoh's social role from CEO of everything, to model devotee of one intangible creative force: the sun.

Akhenaton's 17-year reign produced some lovely works of art and passages of inspiring religious poetry, but little else to compensate Egyptians for the drastic loss of influence their country suffered abroad or the social and economic chaos which prevailed at home. Within 20 years of his death, this heretic pharaoh's monuments were mostly demolished, his innovations repealed, and his very name practically forgotten.[1]

Attempts in later times to force a shining future abruptly into existence have similarly met with failure. Within living memory messianic leaders such as Lenin, Hitler, and Mao Tse Tung, among others, have spread terror, death, and havoc on so great a scale that few today are willing to suggest that any of their policies ever did—or could—produce lasting social benefits.

Future historians will likely modify this judgment somewhat—just as contemporary scholars have rehabilitated Akhenaton, at least in part. Still, it is hard to see how "a better future" will ever be achieved at the expense of widespread human suffering and the damage or destruction of great works of art and other monuments to human creativity. The problem is not change itself, but *impatience* for change.

The record of history suggests that changes are easier to achieve—and more likely to endure—when they are introduced as options rather than as forced commands. A gradual approach allows innovations in technology, work methods, style, and social attitudes to demonstrate their value by competing directly against established norms and practices. As their superiority proves itself, more and more people are persuaded to embrace them freely.

But such a process can take years or even decades—and few reform-minded individuals, whether leaders or followers, are prepared to wait that long. Peaceful but slow progress toward a better future seems to them not a positive achievement but a sign of weakness or shameful compromise. Furthermore, without dramatic evidence of change many reformers lose hope, stop trying to persuade, and seek instead, through violence, to frighten or annihilate those who oppose their plans.

One way to endure living in a less-than-perfect world while still working to improve conditions could be to revise our attitude toward time. Futurists in particular might do well to consider past and future not as opposites, but as eras that overlap, and to recognize that both are uncertain, incomplete, and capable of growth and change.

A New Take on History: in Search of yesterday's tomorrows

At first glance this idea may appear absurd. How can the past change—much less be said to "grow"?

Admittedly futures studies can, at best, do no more than establish the relative probability that one event is more likely than another to occur within a given period of time; while conventional wisdom dictates that the past is "real" and therefore cannot be altered at some later date. And yet the past keeps changing every day.

Historians gain access to previously unknown documents and find they must revise existing histories and biographies to include the new information these disclose. Archeologists are continually turning up new physical evidence that expands our knowledge of past cultures' lifestyles and technologies. Also, shifts in contemporary values frequently cause us to alter our opinions of social movements and leaders of earlier times. Consider the changing status of religious leaders and their followers over time, or, how Americans today regard figures like Jefferson Davis, Kit Carson, Or Christopher Columbus, all of whom were once unchallenged Heroes.

I suggest that there is not just one "true" past any more than there is ever only one "inevitable" future. Surviving records—even when these are detailed and unbiased (which is seldom the case)—tell only part of the story. For the past, like the future, necessarily consists of *possibilities* as well as facts.

Scientists accept that everything they think they know may turn out not to be true. New data, or a new theory that explains existing data better, may compel them to reinterpret axioms long-accepted in their field—as Einstein revolutionized our concept of the universe itself.

Similarly, what we today call "history," is really nothing more that the most convincing theory yet constructed to explain the surviving records and physical evidence that have come down to us from the past. If, as most futurists do, we base our explanations on the premise that human actions are *not* pre-ordained, then comparing all available options is a useful way to decide which policies or actions are most likely to produce desired outcomes. Whatever future actually occurs, it makes sense for planners to consider alternate possibilities in advance.

Taking alternative possibilities into account also makes sense for studying history. Assuming free will exists, then events that *may* have happened (although we lack conclusive evidence for this), or those that *could* have happened (but apparently did not) still represent "real" options, and deserve to be explored. For example, working out alternative lines of history can reveal how different (and from today's perspective, perhaps more favorable) outcomes might have been achieved at moments of decision in the past. It can also suggest how results that we regard today as just and beneficial might have been accomplished by other means, or at lower costs in terms of human suffering and physical destruction.

Alternative history today remains largely a sub-genre of imaginative fiction, and those who write it, like the prolific American author Harry Turtledove, do so primarily to entertain. But some professional historians have begun to take the subject seriously. In *Virtual History: Alternatives and Counter-Factuals* (Basic Books, 2000), Oxford historian Niall Ferguson has explored what he calls "a chaotic theory of the past;" and he concluded his 1999 volume *The Pity of War: Explaining World War I* by reviewing a number of ways in which this "greatest error of modern history" might have been avoided.[2]

Like futures studies itself, serious research into "alternative pasts" may well encounter skepticism and outright opposition within academia. But there are also other ways in which we can use the past to help fashion better futures.

Looking Backward: studying the past

In today's hectic world it is sometimes tempting to act as if history never happened or no longer matters. But it did, and it does. If nothing else, reviewing past events can give one perspective on important issues of the present era. Immediate concerns may frequently seem overwhelming; but how serious are they, really? One way to judge is by comparing them to the threats and conflicts that were upsetting people 10, or 50, or 500 years ago.

Some types of problems keep recurring (*e.g.,* territorial disputes among neighbors, or doctrinal differences between competing factions); but others (*e.g.,* unpopular governments or individual leaders) tend to gradually lose importance or disappear over time. In situations such as these impatience to remove an irritant can often be the spark that turns tension into open violence with unpredictable results.

Instead of rushing to achieve all their goals at once, would-be reformers more familiar with the past might use their knowledge to distinguish between problems that demand immediate action, and others where persuasion, or mere watchfulness, may suffice to preserve stability while promoting steady change. Is it better, for example, to assassinate Napoleon, or Hitler, or Castro, and unleash war in the process; or to plan with patience and be ready to initiate reforms the minute illness or old age has removed the tyrant you oppose?

Those who are suffering right now will likely reject any suggestion that there is a positive value in delay. But they are not thinking like scientists—or futurists. They are simply doing what most human beings do most of the time: thinking with their hearts, their feelings. I suggest that there may be another, better, way.

Neglecting history can actually make desirable futures harder to achieve. Whenever long-familiar landmarks, shared traditions, and conventional wisdom are dismissed as unimportant, people have less reason to care about the future well-being of the place where they live, or about the people who live near them. As cities and regions increasingly lose their distinctive character, and become instead interchangeable sites for trading branded goods and services, traditional loyalties become harder to maintain. If a mushrooming city grows so rapidly that it no longer values its past, who can truly be said to care about its future?

Under such conditions, futures thinking may become an exercise in exclusivity—planning as if only you and those just like you mattered. French architect Le Corbusier's never-realized plan to remake Paris as a series of identical high-rise buildings is one example of this kind of planning. Unfortunately, so are the many massive apartment blocks actually constructed in cities around the globe (particularly to house low-income families) that were directly inspired by Le Corbusier's grandiose design, but ultimately proved to be unlivable.

For a future to have "staying power" it must suit the tastes and values of many more people than just you and those like you. Diversity is no longer an option, it is a necessity; and not only in traditionally tolerant America, but throughout the world. Whatever your personal lifestyle may be, and however much you disapprove of someone else's choices, why assume "*this town* (this planet, this existence) *isn't big enough for both of us?*"

Studying history makes clear how many different sets of values and priorities humans have found worthwhile and satisfying over time. Diversity of language, culture, religion, taste, cuisine, and behavioral norms, not only make life more interesting, they help keep it honest. Technotopia, deep ecology, religious fundamentalism, and secular humanism—just to name a few—all deserve some space within which their adherents can live safe and satisfying lives. Why must any single worldview ever dominate the earth and banish this diversity of dreams?

Instead, let information about each alternative circulate freely among the others, to be tested and debated without pressure or constraint. In time, perhaps one will emerge as the most widely preferred. But it seems just as likely (and perhaps more so) that, given time, unforced experience will demonstrate that different ways of life and sets of values can indeed coexist and flourish side by side, each enriching the other by its presence, and ensuring that people of the future will never lose the opportunity to change their minds.

Wake the Echoes: living the past

Books, pictures, and actual memories all help preserve ideas from the past. But physical contact with the past is what keeps it real. Viewing artifacts on display in museums, touring historic sites, and visiting monuments all help give portions of the past some role in our future. Creating national parks and preserves to protect animals and plants in their wild state performs a similar service for the natural environment. But preservation alone is not an end in itself, and it carries a price.

Like banning development or public access to a wilderness region, designating any site as "historic," is nothing less than an attempt to stop the future dead in its tracks. One generation may believe a certain event or individual has such importance that nothing more significant could possibly happen there. Acting on this belief means pledging ourselves—and every future generation—to spend whatever time, effort, and money it takes to hold back change in this protected place. Such a pledge ought not to be undertaken lightly.

Other choices are possible. For example, instead of saving an entire building, why not be content to set aside some portion of it as a monument to what occurred there, and allow the rest to be adapted for currently useful—and ideally profitable—functions?

This approach has already proven successful. Close to George Washington University in Washington D.C. the attractive façade of one entire block of 19th century buildings was preserved while the interior was transformed from dilapidated homes into a modern shopping center. At a busy crossroads in a nearby suburb, an old electric sign, long a local landmark, has been saved intact and refurbished, even though the restaurant it advertises is now gone. Such a bi-temporal "mixed-use" approach makes contact with the physical past not merely an act of worship—pilgrimage to a shrine—but an experience that brings past and future together. It also makes the cost of long-term preservation less burdensome by building in a method of support. Gift shops and appropriately-themed restaurants at or near historic homes like George Washington's Mount Vernon, or Jefferson's Monticello perform this function too.

The devastation of nature throughout much of the world in modern times and the continuing threats to fragile ecosystems make it tempting to believe that the more acreage we designate as "preserves" the better. Yet, can we safely put our faith in any promise that includes the word "forever"? Even as we legislate new areas "off limits to the future," history warns us that our wishes are unlikely to be honored for very long.

Consider the example of Ancient Egypt. Repeated efforts over 3,000 years to safeguard the tombs of kings and nobles all eventually failed. Within a few decades after burial—and often much sooner—people living near these sites decided they had more to gain by exploiting these resources (in this case, breaking in and stealing treasure) than by laboring loyally to protect them. This same fate could befall our own historic landmark sites and wilderness preserves—particularly if society for any reason should decide to reject our history as no longer relevant or actually harmful to the future.

For example, if America should ever be successfully invaded by a foreign power, would our conquerors continue to honor US historic sites as hallowed ground, or might they not be more inclined to see these as potential rallying spots for resistance, and replace them with monuments to their own heroes and to notable collaborators?

Again, as technologies improve, suppose citizens of some future time decide that a few public parks, some interactive museum displays, and virtual-reality simulations of vanished habitats in cyber-zoos are the only physical contacts with the past they want or need?

My point is not that we should give up trying to protect historic sites or to save the wilderness. I do suggest, however, that we consider exploring options other than "permanent" protection. For example, renewable 100-year leases might be a better choice. These would prevent significant change for the expected lifetimes of all those who approved the decision to protect and preserve in the first place. But it would also allow for periodic reassessment of the original decision.

If we truly feel a duty toward Earth's future citizens, we should try to preserve their options as well as their access to resources. Renewable leases on nature preserves and historic sites would allow later generations to use their own judgment rather than be bound by ours. By deciding for themselves which parks and monuments they believe are still worth preserving for another hundred years, future generations will be voluntarily assuming responsibility for these sites. And they will also know that their descendents, too, will have a chance to reconsider which of their inherited "treasures" are as precious as originally thought, and which might better be released from their enchanted sleep and freed to find a future once again.

Play It Again: experiencing the past

Preserving or respectfully adapting sites for modern use helps keep important evidence from human history available to the future. Likewise, protecting wilderness areas keeps past environments from disappearing. But even these important efforts treat the past as something "static"—set aside to be examined only from a distance. I believe the past can be much more.

A site like Virginia's Colonial Williamsburg, for example, brings people into direct contact with the past through all their senses. Here, amid carefully preserved and restored settings, trained interpreters demonstrate, explain, and allow visitors to experience for themselves how people dressed, ate, worked, and traveled centuries ago.

In recent decades, another way to try and relive the past has emerged: reenacting.

It began in America with efforts to restage battles and troop encampments primarily from the Civil War and Colonial periods. Now the movement to reenact famous events and everyday life experiences from many eras dating back to the Middle Ages and beyond has grown worldwide. In Western Europe, for example, groups meticulously preserve and restore original equipment, uniforms, and vehicles from World War II military units and regularly conduct maneuvers in the field.[3]

But does "reenacting" honor the past or distort it? A focus on unique events and famous individuals can oversimplify history and mix fact with fancy. Too many eager volunteers, combined with the desire to attract free-spending spectators, can easily turn the reenactment of a minor skirmish into a huge outdoor theatrical, featuring units and officers who were nowhere near the original encounter. Moreover, without well-informed and disciplined direction, a reenactment can become just a tailgate party in historical drag. The popular Renaissance Faires, for example, typically include so many mythical and anachronistic elements that visitors cannot distinguish history from entertainment—and, since it's for fun anyway, few even bother to try.[4]

A more authentic way to experience the past firsthand is through "experimental archeology."[5] Here, professional historians and anthropologists guide students and volunteers in efforts to erect a structure, raise crops, or perform other tasks using the same tools and techniques available to people of an earlier time. The goal is not so much to restage famous incidents, but rather, through actual experience, to gain a better understanding of living conditions and work methods believed to have been typical for people living in a particular time and place.

Projects of this kind not only bring the past to life, they also offer an important insight futurists should bear in mind. The past contains far more than just what we call "history." Events judged at the time so extraordinary as to be worth recording for posterity in chronicles are far outnumbered by the wealth of largely unrecorded routine incidents in every era which made up day to day existence. Many of these were no doubt burdensome, repetitive, and dull; but they were also non-threatening, familiar, and ultimately tolerable. Why should we think that life in future times will be any different?

Most futures depicted in science fiction films and stories are far from dull. They tend to feature multi-talented individuals confronting some crisis that can only be resolved by heroic (usually violent) action. Businesses and governments, on the other hand, prefer to deal in soothing fantasies that promise ultimate success through complete control. The scenarios they publish generally assume that ordinary people always act reasonably—or can be induced to do so in their own enlightened self-interest.

While it may be fun to imagine action-filled futures, populated by vicious but vulnerable villains and brave super-heroes, or to plan secure and rational utopias where no one ever rocks the boat—or even tries to, neither vision seems very realistic. Nor do they offer much to inspire enthusiasm in ordinary people more interested in having fun and raising healthy kids than in saving the universe or helping perfect the human race.

Like experimental archeologists, futurists might want to spend a little time exploring details of everyday life in a future world where conditions are neither desperate nor danger-free. For example, while ecologists continue striving to head off catastrophic climate change, it could be useful to imagine and write about—or better yet, to record from personal experience—simple techniques that an average citizen in Western Europe or America might use to cope with long periods of heat or drought in a modern urban setting; or ways for surviving a week-long power blackout.

Clearly, it makes the most sense to avoid such trouble in the first place. But just in case we can't be bothered (or afford) to do so, why must anyone panic or despair when we might get along just fine by adapting some of the attitudes and coping mechanisms that our ancestors employed to "make do" under less than optimal conditions?

"Muddling through" may not be humanity's wisest or most courageous course of action. But it might prove to be one approach that a majority of Earth's inhabitants can understand, accept, and get behind.

Experimental archeology and related research also offer ways to mine the past for resources and knowledge that can benefit the future. In the field of health care, research and rigorous testing of pre-modern treatment methods have already yielded valuable results. From acupuncture and herbal medicine, to the use of obsidian blades in delicate surgery, supposedly "primitive" technologies are once more gaining respect and saving lives.

But why stop here? The past, if we choose, can not only give us back forgotten or neglected wisdom, it can lead us on to wholly new discoveries. Using the tools and methods of past eras, men and women of the future may succeed in answering questions no one thought to ask before.

A New Dispensation: time labs to extend the past

In a sense, we actually "bring the past to life" every time we prepare a meal following an old family recipe, read an out-of-print book, or practice an art or craft employing instruments and skills from an earlier era. The achievements of contemporary artists and craftspeople prove that old materials and methods can be used to do far more than merely "reenact" or duplicate the achievements of the past. In the same way, there is reason to believe that old equipment can be used to produce new findings of value in the natural sciences.

Mathematicians today routinely use computers to save time in making complex calculations. But they can often formulate elegant solutions to puzzling problems using nothing more sophisticated than pencil and paper or chalk on a blackboard. The Wright brothers' bicycle shop contained sufficient resources to produce a successful flying machine. The gaslit, unsterile, poorly-heated laboratories of researchers like Robert Koch and Louis Pasteur were good enough for those who worked in them to develop and verify the efficacy of drugs and treatment methods that have saved countless lives since the 19th century. What new wonders might these same resources generate in the hands of dedicated researchers today?

The nature of the tools available tends to influence what problems scientists select to work on. The fact that giant particle accelerators now exist lures nuclear physicists to devise experiments that will make the fullest possible use of their awesome capabilities. But problems that can only be addressed with the help of the latest and most costly gadgets may not always be the ones most worth exploring. The opportunity to put older lab equipment and "outdated" techniques back in use might stimulate research into problems long forgotten or ignored in the general rush toward technological modernity.

Instead of merely setting up museum replicas of research laboratories from the past, why not reconstruct some of these facilities in full working order and staff them with individuals trained and ready to make appropriate use of their resources? In such "time laboratories" historians of science could guide and instruct students, retired scientists, and volunteers on temporary loan from modern labs, in "old school" methods of research. They might begin by duplicating famous experiments first carried out in similarly equipped laboratories decades or centuries before. Then, as they and their staffs gained expertise and confidence, they could turn their attention to entirely new problems—supplementing the research being carried on in conventional high-tech labs.

The experimental findings obtained in this way could always be checked and verified using state-of-the-art equipment elsewhere. But "time labs" might establish basic principles and promising directions for further study in a variety of fields at lower cost and with fewer outside pressures and distractions than scientists commonly face in university or commercial R&D settings.

Certain challenges in science and technology receive attention because they appear to be timely or seem likely to produce a relatively quick return on investment in the form of patents, prestige, or profitable sales. Thus, in the West, today developing a more powerful vacuum cleaner, a formula for organic toothpaste, or a better sexual stimulant are all attractive lines of research; finding new uses for mud bricks, chick peas, or rock salt, not so much. Yet such relatively cheap and abundant substances may have many more potential uses than we realize today. The example of George Washington Carver, who developed ingenious new products from peanuts, sweet potatoes, and other under-exploited crops, suggests what kinds of research time labs might accomplish.

One more attraction of the time lab process is the possibility that the results of simpler, less narrowly-specialized research might prove easier for government authorities and the general public to accept and appreciate. Consider how many thousands of individuals quickly learned how to repair and customize early automobiles, or mastered the assembly and operation of simple radio equipment. Time labs might specialize in turning out inventions suitable for do-it-yourself construction, operation, and maintenance to help make people less dependent on public services that are vulnerable to disruption from weather or malicious human action.

Endgame Transpositions: getting there from here

Respecting the past, studying it, making it real to our senses, and physically experiencing past conditions as a way to explore new options and possibilities are all actions that could help people choose and create sustainable futures. With adequate attention and investment, the past can provide useful tools, proven techniques, and comprehensible objectives that allow us to easily measure our progress toward desirable ends. Just as decision-makers today often use "backcasting" (positing a goal then working back toward the present to establish a chain of logical steps for achieving that goal), using this same technique from the present to assess past actions and achievements—including credible possibilities for which we, as yet, posses no solid evidence—can help us better understand how today's challenges came into being, and evaluate competing proposals to deal with them.

For futurists, the goal of alternative history—sometimes called "*uchronia*" from the root words "utopia" and "*chronos*" (Greek for "time")—is to identify points where history as we know it might have been modified, how undesirable outcomes might have been avoided, and desirable ones perhaps achieved more quickly or efficiently. In much the same way that chess players learn to recognize when pieces on the board have reached a familiar position known to give one side a distinct advantage, it may even prove possible to spot opportunities for transposition between different historical time lines—because the same desired end result can often be achieved from more than one set of starting conditions.

It may not be possible to turn back the clock and undo past mistakes entirely. But, through careful analysis and planning, much might be done to make up for bad decisions and past setbacks.

One key to a sustainable future world is diversity. We need a future with room for many widely diverging worldviews along with a willingness to share some common ground. Let your personal dream of a desirable future inspire you to action, but don't waste much time criticizing or trying to thwart other people's dreams. Better to keep multiple future dreams alive—even contradictory ones. Let a hundred future visions flower and compete for influence! But be content to win converts by demonstrating your vision's superiority, rather than aggressively attempting to exterminate competitors.

In every life there comes a time when tolerance for diversity is your friend. However dazzling the futures we envision may appear today, they are bound to age—just like our bodies—and in time will come to seem frail, uninspiring, and just plain "old." Let us hope that the world of that time still retains enough tolerance for diversity that it will leave us someplace where we may each stop changing further if we choose, and rest content to enjoy the limited utopia of our own dreaming until, for us, all pasts and futures merge.

—Lane Jennings, Columbia Maryland

*   *   *

Notes

1. A concise overview of Akhenaton and the events of his rule, can be found in *Chronicle of the Pharaohs* by Peter A Clayton (London, 1994), pp. 120-126. For more detail, try *Akhenaton: King of Egypt* by Cyril Aldren (London: 1988).
2. A good introduction to the scope and variety of alternative history today is available at the Uchronia website *www.uchronia.net*.
3. For an introduction to the reenacting movement, check one or more of the following websites: 1) *www.reenactor.net*. This site offers information about historical reenacting around the world; 2) http:members.tripod.com/~majladiv/number1.html>. This site, produced by Stevan Martin, offers links to many U.S. groups seeking individuals interested in Civil War reenacting; 3) *www.panzerdivision.org*,. This World War II reenactor group strongly disavows "any activity that can be interpreted as public support for fascism." It is worth remembering that taking part in a reenactment does not imply endorsing the motives, behavior, or worldview of the people of that time.

4. For more information about Renaisssance Faires and similar events check *www.sca.org*, (The Society for Creative Anachronism) which describes itself as "an international organization dedicated to researching and recreating the arts and skills of pre-seventeenth-century Europe."

5. For a brief but helpful overview of this subject, see the Wikipedia website: *http://en.wikipedia.org/wiki/Experimental_archaeology.*

EXCHANGES

AND

COLLABORATIONS

Cross-Generational Conversations and Parallels in Verse

TWO EROTIC ESSAYS SPANNING 80 YEARS

IN THE LANE (ca. 1905)

There's a lane I know where daisies grow
        And the alder blossoms fair;
Where youths and maidens often go
To gather the violets that show
Among the hedges there.

Odors of sweetbriar, mint and thyme
        Freshen that path so green;
Soft the gentle breezes blow,
And soft the trailing willows bow,
Stirred by a hand unseen.

The name of the place is *Friendship Lane*,
        And it leads to the highway, *Love*;
Full many an unsuspecting pair
Have innocently wandered there
While blue skies arched above.

Many a couple those ways have trod,
        Where the lane breathes odors sweet,
Till, lingering lightly, man and maid,
They come to a stop where the lane's
cool shade
Gives way to the highway's heat.

Happy the pair who will dare the day
        And embark on that highway broad;
But many, faint-hearted, turn away,
Reluctant to leave their easy play,
And never find the road.

—**William Silver Jennings**

ILLICIT VALENTINE (ca. 1985)

Wise and shy
        you and I
        as we
in twining minds
        led lives
        of quiet aspiration.

Ruly passions
        schooled us
        to their use,
but did not dull
        our just desires.

Sleeping fires
        lay
        deposited
in banks
        of glowing coals
accumulating
    interest
        night
                        by
                                night.

            Now . . .
here we are
the vault's ajar,
and this
(my stealthy darling)
        is a stickup!

—**Lane Eaton Jennings**

LUCKLESS

Variations on a Theme
By three generations

A Luckless Wight

By William S. Jennings

A luckless wight be I this night,
    My heart is troubled sore;
Two maids I love with all my might,
And 'twere in truth a puzzling plight
    If there were any more

Now Daphne, beauteous queen is she;
She garbs herself so splendidly
That people turn again to see
    When she goes down the street.
Her plumes they wave, her ribbons fly,
Her wondrous hair is piled so high,
And she hath such a majesty
    My heart is at her feet.

But Phoebe's jaunty cap is white,
Her apron is a fetching sight
When she doth serve the tea at night,
    And she is fair to see.
Her biscuits are beyond compare,
Her cakes they be as light as air,
And with her magic everywhere
    She captivateth me.

Oh, am I not a luckless wight
    Perplexed thus to be?
I love them both with all my might,
And faith, it is a vexing plight,
    For neither one loves me.

Luckless Redux

By Robert K. Jennings

I weep for you, my Father dear!
    I deeply sympathize.
I, too, have loved what might appear
Ideal mates for my career
    Who would NOT be my wives.

Now. 'sposing Daphne DID agree
Your bride she after all would be
(In raiment fetched from gay Paree)—
    Well, can the lady cook?
And can she type, and scrub, and sew,
Bail out the dinghy while you row,
And make the kitchen garden grow?
    (You'd have to sell a book!)

Or Phoebe. Would she really be
An asset in society?
(A kitchen paragon is she,
    But would she grace your table?)
A phoebe (so I've always heard)
Is such a drab, retiring bird.
The perfect hostess? How absurd!
    Willing but quite unable!

I'd say things turned out quite all right
    You married sweet Irene!
A loving lass; a pleasing sight
('T would otherwise have been MY plight
    For I'd
        Have never been!)

LW3

(with a bow—and apologies—to WSJ and RKJ)
By Lane E. Jennings

I feel for dad, and grandpa Will,
        Who loved (alas, in vain)
Two girls. Like them, I've felt that thrill—
Now up, now down, now through the mill—
        The doubt, the joy, the pain.

One look, you're smitten, sure as fate!
You ask her out, you dine, you date.
Then, just when things are going great,
        She suddenly turns prim.
The same thing happens more than once.
Don Juan you're not—but you're no dunce.
Truth dawns: You're NOT the one she wants!
        She'd rather be with HIM.

Another try: a girl with wits,
It's more than just her shapely tits,
More than the part on which she sits,
        That takes your mind off dinner.
Her skill at repartee and jest,
Her daddy's well-filled treasure chest,
His friends: the brightest and the best!
        (You woo, but fail to win her).

Trumped once again, jack falls to queen.
        Fate has another plan.
As Bob found his Edith; Will, Irene;
True love at last came on the scene
        When I found
                Cheryl Ann!

EXPERIENCE AND DISCOVERY:
More Variations on a Theme

MY SONG

by William S. Jennings (1918)

I searched my soul for a song of cheer
When the candle flickered low,
But brooding shadows hovered near,
A whimpering night owl tried my ear,
The wet wind sighed in the darkness drear,
And my rhymes were lame and slow.

I walked at dawn where the dew was deep,
And the tuneful treetops rang.
I saw the forager squirrel leap,
The minnows flashed where the sun did peep,
The morning-glories awoke form sleep,
And my soul arose and sang.

COMMONPLACE

by Robert K. Jennings (1944)

I prayed the Lord might let me view
The peace and grandeur angels know:
And when I woke, the world was new
All furbished with fresh-fallen snow.

I begged a miracle, as proof
That God was not a hope forlorn:
I prayed, and lo, beneath my roof
A child was born.

ANSWERED PRAYERS

by Lane E. Jennings (2008)

I looked for love, and passionate play
When I was young and pleasure-bound.
I trusted winning words
Would turn the world around.

Companionship, and sympathy,
Patience, and peace, were what I found;
And worth the wait, once time
Had turned *my* world around.

LINEAGE* (1988-2012)

A Collaboration by Father and Son Poets
Robert K. and Lane E. Jennings

Following eternal rules
Atoms align as molecules—

Form *Homo sapiens*, modern man,
Establish gender, race, and clan.

By family traits, familiar ones,
We know ourselves our fathers' sons

Through slant of eyebrow, cheek, and nose,
Skin, eyes, and hair, acceptance grows.

Gene-ings of long-forgotten *"Jan"*
The Nominator of our clan,

Whose syllable and spark we blend
Till powers fail and namings end.

Deeper than history can reach
Extends our kinship each to each—

e pluribus Jennings!
Ever on . . .

As David treasured Absalom
So Levi doted on Clarkson,

As Clarkson then adored his Will,
So William cherished Bob—until

Bob sired baby Lane; and lo,
He found him good—or nearly so.

Today no Jennings men remain
Except Will's only grandson: Lane.

That father-feeling, flowing bright,
From out the misty ancient night

Dies here with me. Yet, childless, I
Long to pass on, before I die

Some good of them that might be shared:
Three generations' voices paired

For good—for better, or for worse—
In pleasant prose and supple verse.

Grandfather, father, only son
Are flesh made word, and so live on

Paper patriarchs in a line:
Letters their lineage—and mine.

Through each a flood of feeling comes:
Spun out in lines . . .

Love's chromosomes?

—

*[from an unfinished RKJ original dated 1988; revised by LJ 1997 and after]

CLOSING LINES

from **THE VOYAGE** <small>(ca.1920)</small>

By William S. Jennings

. . . Out in the west the evening sun
Flooded the sky with a golden light,
As softly and silently, one by one,
Three battered vessels came home at night,
And brought the fruits of the voyage there,
The wealth of the lads so young and fair
Who had sailed in the early morning.

from **THE WEAVING OF THE STOLE** <small>(ca. 1946)</small>

By Robert K. Jennings

. . . And so each serves, and who may say how well?
Each ties his knot into History's spreading lace—
A large or tiny heritage to tell
The Future of his sojourn in that space.
But here and there a brilliant jewel is sewn,
By those who worked for gain—but not their own.

THE WAY IT IS (ca. 1972)

By Lane E. Jennings

With no illusions
we arrived
in the land of
those-who-don't-read-poetry.
And we

wrote poetry
with no illusions
for the land
of those who don't read poetry
to read

Title Index

All listed items are poems except titles in italics are short stories and those in quotation marks are non-fiction articles

Index of First Lines

(Poems only)

Bibliography

The citations listed here do not include all publications by these authors, but provide some indication of the kinds of readers each one managed to reach.

William Silver Jennings (1877-1924)

Poems
Phyllis Hath My Heart in Tow first appeared in *The Ladies World* for Oct. 1910
Other poems appeared in *The Indiana Farmer's Guide*, etc.

Stories
Adoniram Retreats appeared in *The Canadian Countryman*, June 1915
He also published short fiction in *All Stories Weekly, Farm and Fireside, Little Folks Magazine, The Youth's Companion*, etc.

Robert Kimmel Jennings (1912-1996)

Poems
Friends' Meeting appeared in *Clear Horizons* 1948
The Judgment Seat first appeared in *St. Anthony Messenger* for May, 1947
For several years during the late 1940s RKJ wrote a regular column called "Sermons in Verse" for the magazine *Front Rank*. He also published poems in *The Albatross, Different, Good Business, Media Comment*, etc.

Stories
Why the Loon Laughs appeared in *What to Do: The Boys and Girls Weekly* for 4 October 1948

Lane Eaton Jennings (b. 1944)

Poems
Cupid with Spear Gun appeared in *Treasure House*, 1985
Not Ungrateful in *The Christian Science Monitor* 17 Nov 1983
Unbecoming Verse in *Nebula* 6, Fall 1977
Omar Khayyam and the Voyager Probes in *Visions* 12, 1983
Shakespearean Brag in *Visions* 20, 1986

Moonrise on I-95 in *Little Patuxent Review*, #4 1981
Creature Comforts in *Antietam Review* 2005
To His Cool Mistress in the anthology *The Ear's Chamber*, ed. Stacy
Tuthill 1981
Stars in the anthology *Weavings*, ed. Michael Glaser, 2000
Other poems have appeared in *Amelia, Bitterroot, Bogg, Catalyst, Gargoyle,
Green Mountain Review, Starline, Third Wind*, etc.

Stories
Sagesse Oblige (2010) and *Cras Amet* (2011) were both first published
in the online journal *Praxilla*.

www.ingramcontent.com/pod-product-compliance
Lightning Source LLC
LaVergne TN
LVHW090434170825
818615LV00002B/13